D1242078

HENRY THOREAU

As Remembered by a Young Friend

Edward Waldo Emerson

DOVER PUBLICATIONS, INC.
Mineola, New York

Bibliographical Note

This Dover edition, first published in 1999, is an unabridged republication of the work originally published by Houghton Mifflin Company, Boston, in 1917. The Introduction and footnotes were prepared for the Dover edition.

Library of Congress Cataloging-in-Publication Data

Emerson, Edward Waldo, 1844–1930.
  Henry Thoreau as remembered by a young friend / Edward Waldo Emerson.
      p.   cm.
  Originally published: Boston : Houghton, Mifflin, 1917. With new introd.
  ISBN 0-486-40896-5 (pbk.)
    1. Thoreau, Henry David, 1817–1862—Friends and associates.
  2. Authors, American—19th century—Biography.   I. Title.
PS30503.E45   1999
818'.309—dc21
  [B]   99–34268
                                                                    CIP

Manufactured in the United States of America
Dover Publications, Inc., 31 East 2nd Street, Mineola, N.Y. 11501

Introduction to the Dover Edition

IN September 1844, Ralph Waldo Emerson announced to his friend Thomas Carlyle several recent changes in the Emerson household: the birth of a son the previous summer and the purchase of some land adjacent to Emerson's property in Concord:

Edward we call him, & my wife calls him Edward Waldo. When shall I show him to you? And when shall I show you a pretty pasture & woodlot which I bought last week on the borders of a lake which is the chief ornament of this town called Walden Pond? One of these days, if I should have any money, I may build me a cabin or a turret there high as the treetops and spend my nights as well as days in the midst of a beauty which never fades for me.

It was not Emerson, of course, who built a retreat next to Walden Pond; it was instead his young friend and neighbor, Henry David Thoreau, who, on the fourth of July, 1845, took up residence in a one-room house he had built with his own hands (and very little money) and began a quiet and far-reaching revolution of personal independence.

A graduate of Harvard in 1837, Thoreau had returned after college to his native village, where he attempted to solve the practical problems of life with as little interference to his spiritual and intellectual well-being as was possible for mankind following Adam's fall from grace. He sometimes helped out in the family business of pencil making; he taught at two schools; he offered his services as surveyor when needed; and he did various odd jobs around the town. It seemed remarkable to his fellow citizens in

Concord that he so utterly lacked ambition in the ways of worldly success that he refused to fulfill the promise that even in those times a Harvard education practically guaranteed. Even Emerson failed in large part to appreciate the profound virtues of Thoreau's life decisions, and he later chastised his friend for refusing to take command, for refusing to embark upon some great enterprise for the betterment of society. Or as Emerson succinctly put it: "instead of engineering for all America, he was the captain of a huckleberry-party."

But Emerson's son Edward knew better. During the two years he resided by Walden Pond, Thoreau frequently visited the Emersons and became to the children like "a delightful older brother, a good uncle." When, in 1847, Emerson decided to make a long stay in Europe, it was decided that Thoreau should move in during his absence to look after the family, and on the sixth of September, Thoreau left his shelter by the shores of Walden Pond and settled in the Emerson house on Lexington Road. Edward, now three, was delighted, as were his two older sisters. But they were not the only ones. A few weeks following Emerson's departure, Thoreau wrote to the absent master of the house about life with Mrs. Emerson, the three children, and Lidian Emerson's sister, Lucy Jackson Brown:

Lidian and I make very good housekeepers. She is a very dear sister to me. Ellen and Edith and Eddy and Aunty Brown keep up the tragedy and comedy and tragic-comedy of life as usual. The two former have not forgotten their old acquaintance; even Edith carries a young memory in her head, I find. Eddy can teach us all how to pronounce. If you should discover any rare hoard of wooden or pewter horses, I have no doubt he will know how to appreciate it. He occasionally surveys mankind from my shoulders as wisely as ever [Dr. Samuel] Johnson did. I respect him not a little, though it is I that lift him up so unceremoniously. And sometimes I have to set him down again in a hurry, according to his "mere will and good pleasure." He very seriously asked me, the other day, "Mr. Thoreau, will you be my father?" I am occasionally Mr. Rough-and-tumble with him that I may not miss *him*, and lest he should miss *you* too much. So you must come back soon, or you will be superseded.

Emerson was relieved to know that his family was in safe hands, writing to his wife that "our Spartan-Buddhist Henry is a "*Père* or *bon-homme malgré lui,* and it is a great comfort daily to think of him there with you."

Upon Emerson's return ten months later, Thoreau moved back to his own father's house, but he remained an intimate of the Emerson family circle. He continued to be particularly close to the children, who looked upon the older man as a sort of Pied Piper whose magic whistle opened the imaginations of youth to the wonders and mysteries of the natural world. As Edward recalled in his memoir: "He soon became the guide and companion of our early expeditions afield, and, later, the advisor of our first camping trips." The friendship lasted through the boy's youth, and when Edward was seventeen and about to enter Harvard, Thoreau took the young man aside and assured him that he would never be far from home, predicting that following Edward's college days he "would return home and live out his days in his beloved Concord," just as Thoreau had done.

The return home for Edward was far more difficult than either of them could have imagined. The burden of being his father's son rested heavily upon Edward's shoulders, and circumstances and family expectations often thwarted his ambitions and personal desires. Almost unspoken in his early days was his wish to be an artist (the elder Emerson pointed out that this was no way to earn the living expected of him). His frail constitution prevented him from enlisting during the early months of the Civil War, a great disappointment that never lessened with the years, and, soon after, he failed in the railroad business in the West. Finally settling on medicine, and studying at Harvard and in Germany, he became a country doctor in his native village, a profession he did good service in for nine years but never truly enjoyed.

When he found financial independence following his father's death in 1882, Edward left medicine and turned to his first passion, painting. But it was too late, and besides, his talents were limited. During the next several decades he busied himself with various literary projects: writing a memoir of *Emerson in Concord* (1889), annotating his father's *Works* for the important Centenary Edition (1903–4), and editing in ten volumes Emerson's *Journals* (1909–14). In addition he wrote lives of Charles Russell Lowell, a Harvard classmate who served heroically in the Civil War (1907), and of his father's friend, Ebenezer Rockwood Hoar (1911); and he compiled a record of *The Early Years of the Saturday Club* (1918), the Boston dinner club that had dominated the literary and social life of the region during the middle years of the 19th century but that by the early 20th century seemed to many to be provincial, anachronistic. In short, it was a career defined largely by the achievements of others, a life of compromises and, in the words of Bliss Perry, "of second choices." He earned appropriate rewards; being honored as a respected citizen and civic leader in Concord, a member of the Massachusetts Historical Society, a fellow of the American Academy of Arts and Sciences, a good man and faithful husband.

As keeper of the traditions and values of the lost world of Concord, Edward Emerson was drawn repeatedly back to the example of Thoreau, perhaps seeing in his old friend's refusal to settle for mere worldly success a quiet rebuke of his own need at one time to win his father's approval and a place in the social world. However, it was not Thoreau the stoic or the mystic whom Emerson remembered, but rather the "kindly and affectionate person" so loved by the children of the town.

Toward the end of the 19th century Thoreau was emerging from the obscurity of Concord lore and beginning to assume the mythic-symbolic dimensions that have largely defined his role in the American cultural imagination during the 20th century. Emerson felt that truth was being sacrificed for the convenience of the fictions of history. In particular, he objected to the familiar portraits drawn of his early mentor and friend by James Russell Lowell, Robert Louis Stevenson, and others that revealed a humorless, cold individual, "devoid," in Stevenson's words, "of any quality of flesh and blood." During the 1890s Emerson lectured a number of times on Thoreau, in Concord as well as in New York and London, and when the 1917 centennial anniversary of Thoreau's birth approached he turned the material into the book we have here. In addition to his own recollections, Edward Emerson drew upon the reminiscences of others in Concord who had known him, including some of Thoreau's former pupils, whose memories might otherwise have gone unrecorded.

Emerson's book has remained ever since its publication an important tool in the understanding of Thoreau's complex character. In the words of Walter Harding, perhaps the most knowledgeable of Thoreau's modern biographers, "As a portrait of Thoreau the human being, this little volume has not been excelled. It refutes those who would dismiss Thoreau as a misanthrope, for the person who emerges from these pages is warm, friendly, kind, and genial." Or as a reviewer wrote in *The Dial* at the time of the book's publication in 1917: "These illuminating glimpses of a strongly marked and splendidly independent but too often misunderstood personality are a welcome addition to the rather meagre literary product called forth by the Thoreau centennial. In this little book Thoreau the idealist stands justified for his refusal to devote the best years of his life to pencil-making and money-getting."

Thomas Wortham
Chair and Professor of American
Literature, U.C.L.A.

Preface

I CAN remember Mr. Thoreau as early as I can remember anybody, excepting my parents, my sisters, and my nurse. He had the run of our house, and on two occasions was man of the house during my father's long absences. He was to us children the best kind of an older brother. He soon became the guide and companion of our early expeditions afield, and, later, the advisor of our first camping trips. I watched with him one of the last days of his life, when I was about seventeen years old.

Twenty-seven years ago I was moved to write a lecture, now taking form in this book, because I was troubled at the want of knowledge and understanding, both in Concord and among his readers at large, not only of his character, but of the events of his life,—which he did not tell to everybody,—and by the false impressions given by accredited writers who really knew him hardly at all. Mr. Lowell's[†] essay on Thoreau is by no means worthy of the subject, and has unhappily prejudiced many persons against him.

When I undertook to defend my friend, I saw that I must at once improve my advantage of being acquainted, as a country doctor, with many persons who would never put pen to a line, but knew much about him—humble persons whom the literary men would never find out, like those who helped in the pencil mill, or in a survey,[††] or families whom he came to know well and value in his walking over every square rod of Concord, or one of the brave and humane managers of the Underground Railroad, of which Thoreau was an operative. Also I had the

---

[†]James Russell Lowell (1819–91), poet and critic.
[††]Thoreau worked as a land surveyor in Concord.

good fortune to meet or correspond with six of the pupils of Thoreau and his brother John, all of whom bore witness to the very remarkable and interesting character of the teachers and their school.

Indeed, a half-century in advance of his time was Thoreau's attitude in many matters, as the change in thought and life in New England fifty years after his death shows. Of course, the people of that day went to temperance picnics, went fishing and huckleberrying and picked flowers, and enjoyed outdoors to that extent, and a very few took walks in the woods; but Thoreau, by the charm of his writings, led many young people to wood walks and river journeys, without gun or rod, but for the joy of out-of-doors in all the seasons in their splendor. A whole literature of this kind has sprung up since his day, unquestionably inspired by him. Nature study is in all the schools. The interesting and original methods of teaching during the last thirty years recall those of the brothers; and where is corporal punishment?

As to the pencil business. I wish to show his dutiful and respectful attitude toward his family, and the important part he bore in improving their lead-pencil business and putting it for the time beyond competition in this country, giving them a good maintenance; although "his life was too valuable to him to put into lead-pencils." Suppose he had done so?

I wish to show that Thoreau, though brusque on occasions, was refined, courteous, kind and humane; that he had a religion and lived up to it.

"If you build castles in the air," he said, "that is where they should be. Now put the foundations under them."

EDWARD WALDO EMERSON

CONCORD, May 1917

Illustrations

An instinct, perhaps inherited, prompts me to introduce my subject with a text.

A Greek author, centuries ago, left these words behind, but not his name:

"You ask of the gods health and a beautiful old age; but your tables are opposed to it; they fetter the hands of Zeus."

I shall use yet another text; Wordsworth's lines:

> "Yet was Rob Roy as wise as brave—
> Forgive me if that phrase be strong—
> A poet worthy of Rob Roy
> Must scorn a timid song."

In childhood I had a friend,—not a house friend, domestic, stuffy in association; nor yet herdsman, or horseman, or farmer, or slave of bench, or shop, or office; nor of letters, nor art, nor society; but a free, friendly, youthful-seeming man, who wandered in from unknown woods or fields without knocking,—

> "Between the night and day
> When the fairy king has power,"—

as the ballad says, passed by the elders' doors, but straightway sought out the children, brightened up the wood-fire forthwith; and it seemed as if it were the effect of a wholesome brave north wind, more than of the armful of "cat-sticks" which he would bring in from the yard. His type was Northern,—strong features, light brown hair, an open-air complexion with suggestion of a seafaring race; the mouth pleasant and flexible when he spoke, aquiline nose, deep-set but very wide-open eyes of clear blue grey, sincere, but capable of a twinkle, and again of austerity, but not of softness. Those eyes could not be made to rest on what was unworthy, saw much and keenly (but yet in certain worthy directions hardly at all), and did not fear the face of clay. A figure short and narrow, but thick; a carriage assuring of sturdy strength and endurance. When he walked to get over the ground one thought of a tireless machine, seeing his long, direct, uniform pace; but his body was active and well balanced, and his step could be light, as of one who could leap or dance or skate well at will.

His dress was strong and plain. He was not one of those little men who try to become great by exuvial methods of length of hair or beard, or broad collars, or conspicuous coat.

This youthful, cheery figure was a familiar one in our house, and when he, like the "Pied Piper of Hamelin," sounded his note in the hall, the children must needs come and hug his knees, and he struggled with them, nothing loath, to the fireplace, sat down and told stories, sometimes of the strange adventures of his childhood, or more often of squirrels, muskrats, hawks, he had seen that day, the Monitor-and-Merrimac duel of mud-turtles in the river, or the great Homeric battle of the red and black ants. Then he would make our pencils and knives disappear, and redeem them presently from our ears and noses; and last, would bring down the heavy copper warming-pan from the oblivion of the garret and unweariedly shake it over the blaze till reverberations arose within, and then opening it, let a white-blossoming explosion of popcorn fall over the little people on the rug.

Later, this magician appeared often in house or garden and always to charm.

Another tells of a picture that abides with her of this figure standing at the door of a friend, with one foot on the great stone step, surrounded by eager listeners, for he had just been seeing the doings, and hearing the songs, not of dull and busy workers,—great stupid humans,—but of those they above all desired to know about, the strange and shy dwellers in the deep woods and along the rivers.

Surely a True Thomas of Ercildoune returned from his stay in Faërie with its queen's gift of a "tongue that shall never lie."

And yet another tells how, though this being sometimes looked uncouth to her, like a "'long-shore-man,"—she could never quite forgive the sin that his garments sat strangely on him,—when he told his tale to the ring of children it was, as it were, a defence, for he seemed abashed by them. Perhaps as the years came on him he began to feel with the sad Vaughan[†] concerning childhood—

[†] Henry Vaughan, Welsh poet (1621?–1695).

"I cannot reach it, and my striving eye[1]
  Dazzles at it, as at Eternity";

and his hope was with him to keep

  "that innocence alive,
  The white designs that children drive."

And it was this respect for unspoiled nature in the creatures of
the wood that was his passport to go into their dwelling-places
and report to the children that were like enough to them to care
to hear.

This youth, who could pipe and sing himself, made for children
pipes of all sorts, of grass, of leaf-stalk of squash and pumpkin,
handsome but fragrant flageolets of onion tops, but chiefly of
the golden willow-shoot, when the rising sap in spring loosens
the bark. As the children grew older, he led them to choice
huckleberry hills, swamps where the great high-bush blueberries
grew, guided to the land of the chestnut and barberry, and more
than all, opened that land of enchantment into which, among
dark hemlocks, blood-red maples, and yellowing birches, we
floated in his boat, and freighted it with leaves and blue gentians
and fragrant grapes from the festooning vines.

A little later, he opened another romantic door to boys full
of Robin Hood; made us know for ourselves that nothing was
truer than

  "'T is merry! 't is merry in the good green wood
  When mavis and merle are singing!"—

told us how to camp and cook, and especially how, at still mid-
night, in the middle of Walden, to strike the boat with an oar,—
and, in another minute, the hills around awoke, cried out, one
after another with incredible and startling *crash*, so that the
Lincoln Hill and Fairhaven, and even Contantum, took up the
tale of the outrage done to their quiet sleep. He taught us also
the decorum and manners of the wood, which gives no treasures
or knowledge to the boisterous and careless; the humanity not
to kill a harmless snake because it was ugly, or in revenge for a

start; and that the most zealous collector of eggs must always leave the mother-bird most of her eggs, and not go too often to watch the nest.

He showed boys with short purses, but legs stout, if short, how to reach the nearer mountains,—Wachusett, then Monadnoc,—and live there in a bough-house, on berries and meal and beans, happy as the gods on Olympus, and like them, in the clouds and among the thunders.

He always came, after an expedition afar, to tell his adventures and wonders, and all his speech was simple and clean and high. Yet he was associated with humble offices also, for, like the friendly Troll in the tale, he deftly came to the rescue when any lock or hinge or stove needed the hand of a master.

I saw this man ever gravely and simply courteous, quietly and effectively helpful, sincere, always spoken of with affection and respect by my parents and other near friends;—knew him strongly but not noisily interested on the side of Freedom in the great struggle that then stirred the country.

When the red morning began to dawn in Kansas and at Harper's Ferry,[†] I saw him deeply moved, and though otherwise avoiding public meetings and organized civic action, come to the front and, moved to the core, speak among the foremost against oppression.

Fatal disease laid hold on him at this time and I saw him face his slow death with cheerful courage.

Then I went away from home, and began to read his books; but in the light of the man I knew. I met persons who asked questions about him, had heard strange rumours and made severe criticisms; then I read essays and satires, even by one whose gifts render such obtuseness well-nigh unpardonable,[2] in which he was held lightly or ridiculed—heard that he was pompous, rustic, conceited, that his thoughts were not original, that he strove to imitate another; that even his observations on natural history were of no value, and not even new.

Even in Concord among persons who had known him slightly at

---

†Pre-Civil War violent struggles between proslavery and Abolitionist forces.

school or in the young society of his day, or had some acquaintance with him in village relations, I found that, while his manifest integrity commanded respect, he was regarded unsympathetically by many, and not only the purposes, but many of the events of his life were unknown. The indictments are numerous, but of varying importance:—When a school-teacher, he once flogged several pupils at school without just cause. Once some wood-lots were burned through his carelessness. He carried a tree through the town while the folks came home from meeting. He, while living at Walden, actually often went out to tea, and carried pies home from his mother's larder. He let others pay his taxes. He was lazy. He was selfish. He did not make money, as he might have done for himself and family by attending to his business. He did not believe in Government and was unpatriotic. He was irreligious.

What, then, was Thoreau?

The man of whom I speak was the friend of my childhood and early youth, and living and dead has helped me, and in no common way. It is a natural duty, then, to acknowledge thankfully this help and render homage to his memory, because his name and fame, his life and lesson, have become part of America's property and are not merely the inheritance of the children who dwell by the Musketaquid.[†]

Three of his friends have already written of him, yet I can add to their testimony, explain and illustrate some things more fully. Also I have gleaned in Concord homes and fields from others, now dead, who would never have written them, memories that might soon have faded away, and have done what I may to preserve them. To many persons he is but a name, or a character pictured by artists of varying skill, sometimes unsympathetic, if not unfriendly. Yet I will say alike to all, Let us fairly review the ground you perhaps deem well known, and see if with the light of the latter years, and the better perspective, you may not find values there, passed by as nought in earlier years.

---

†A river that flowed by Concord.

David Henry Thoreau (his baptismal names were afterward transposed) was born in a farmhouse on the "Virginia Road," a mile and a half east of the village, July 2, 1817. Next year the family moved to Chelmsford, then to Boston, where his schooling began. They returned to Concord when he was six years old, and remained there.

Pleasant pictures remain of the children and the home. The father, John Thoreau, whose father came from the Isle of Jersey, was a kindly, quiet man, not without humour, who, though a canny and not especially ambitious mechanic, was intelligent and always tried to give good wares to his customers. He and his wife knew Concord woods thoroughly, and first led their children into them to study birds and flowers. The mother, Cynthia Dunbar, of Scotch ancestry, was spirited, capable, and witty, with an edge to her wit on occasion, but there is abundant and hearty testimony from many of her neighbours—to which I can add my own—to her great kindness, especially to young people, often shown with much delicacy; also to her thoughtfulness and her skill in making home pleasant, even on the smallest capital, by seasoning spare diet and humble furnishings by native good taste, and, more than all, by cheerfulness; for this good woman knew how to keep work and care in their proper places, and give life and love the precedence. A near neighbour and friend told me that for years the family had on ordinary days neither tea, coffee, sugar, nor other luxuries, that the girls might have the piano which their early musical taste showed they would want, and the education of all, especially the sending of the younger son to college, might be provided for; and yet her table was always attractive, and the food abundant and appetizing. There were two daughters and two sons, of whom Henry was the younger.[3]

This little picture of Henry Thoreau's childhood survives, told by his mother to an old friend: John and Henry slept together in the trundlebed, that obsolete and delightful children's bed, telescoping on large castors under the parental four-poster. John would go to sleep at once, but Henry often lay long awake. His mother found the little boy lying so one night, long after he had gone upstairs, and said, "Why, Henry dear, why don't you go to sleep?" "Mother," said he, "I have been looking through the stars to see if I couldn't see God behind them."

Henry prepared himself for Harvard College in the Concord schools. Out of hours he attended the dame-school taught by Nature. She smoothed the way from the village by ice or glassy water, or baited the footpath to the woods with berries, and promised fabulous beasts and birds and fishes to the adventuring boy with box-trap, fish-hook, or flint-lock shotgun. With these Thoreau was very expert, though he early passed through that grade in this academy and left them behind. All of the family had out-of-door instincts, and the relation of the children to their parents and each other was unusually happy and harmonious.

He had such opportunities for formal spiritual training as were then afforded by the Unitarian and Orthodox churches in Concord, at both of which his family attended worship.

The comparatively small amount which it then cost to maintain a boy at Harvard (which, it must be remembered, strange as it may sound, was, and is, a charitable institution), was enough seriously to strain the resources of the family. The mother had saved for the emergency, as has been said, the older sister helped, the aunts reinforced, and Henry helped by winning and keeping a scholarship and (as was the wholesome custom of the day for a large proportion of the students) by teaching school for periods during the College course. But, thinking over the sacrifices, I was told, by a friend of his mother's, that he said that the result was not worth the outlay and the sacrifice it had called for.

Evidence of independence and character appear in his student life. Though an unusually good student of the classics and of mathematics, as his after use of these studies fully proves, he saw that the *curriculum* was narrow, and to make the sacrifice worth while he must not stick too closely to it, lured by College rank and honours and the chance of making a figure at Commencement. So believing, even although the loss of marks involved nearly cost the important relief of a scholarship and brought some disapproval of his teachers, he deliberately devoted much of his time to the College library—an opportunity and prize to a country boy who knew how to avail himself of it in those days, which now, when public and private libraries are common, it is hard to realize; and he acquired there a knowledge of good authors remarkable then or now. When I went to College he counselled me that the library was perhaps the best gift Harvard had to offer, and through life he constantly used it, braving the bull-dog official that foolish custom kept there to keep the books useless, and when he was surly, going at once to the College authorities and obtaining special privileges as a man not to be put aside when in the right.

He graduated in 1837 with fair rank and an excellent character and received the degree of Bachelor of Arts.[4]

Highly interesting it is to find that Thoreau at twenty, in his "Part" at Commencement, pleaded for the life that, later, he carried out. An observer from the stars, he imagines, "of our planet and the restless animal for whose sake it was contrived, where he found one man to admire with him his fair dwelling-place, the ninety and nine would be scraping together a little of the gilded dust upon its surface. . . .

"Let men, true to their natures, cultivate the moral affections, lead manly and independent lives; . . . The sea will not stagnate, the earth will be as green as ever, and the air as pure. This curious world which we inhabit is more wonderful than it is convenient; more beautiful than it is useful; it is more to be admired and enjoyed than used. The order of things should be somewhat reversed; the seventh should be man's day of toil, wherein to earn his living by the sweat of his brow; and the other six his Sabbath of the affections and the soul,—in which to range this widespread garden, and drink in the soft influences and sublime revelations of Nature."

To teach was the work that usually offered itself to the hand of a country youth fresh from college. Failing to find at once a better opportunity afar, Thoreau took charge of the Town School in Concord, but, it is said, proving heretical as to Solomon's maxim concerning the rod, did not satisfy the Committeeman, who was a deacon. Deacon ——— sat through one session with increasing disapproval, waiting for corporal chastisement, the corner-stone of a sound education, and properly reproved the teacher. The story which one of Thoreau's friends told me was, that with a queer humour,—he was very young,—he, to avoid taking the town's money, without giving the expected equivalent, in the afternoon punished six children, and that evening resigned the place where such methods were required. One of the pupils, then a little boy, who is still living, all through life has cherished his grievance, not understanding the cause. But we may be sure his punishment would not have been cruel, for Henry Thoreau always liked and respected children. Later this pupil came to know and like him. He said "he seemed the sort of a man that wouldn't willingly hurt a fly," and, except on this occasion, had shown himself mild and kindly.

But next year began a different sort of teaching. John and Henry took the Concord Academy. John was the principal, perhaps twenty-three years old, of pleasant face, gay, bright, sympathetic, while the more original and serious younger brother was, I think, troubled with consciousness, and though very human, undemonstrative. He mainly took charge of the classical department. Twenty-seven years ago I had the fortune to talk or correspond with six of their pupils and found that all remembered the school pleasantly, several with enthusiasm, and in their accounts of it, the influence of the character of the teachers and the breadth and quality of the instruction appear remarkable. One scholar[5] said: "It was a peculiar school, there was never a boy flogged or threatened, yet I never saw so absolutely military discipline. How it was done I scarcely know. Even the incorrigible were brought into line."

This scholar, who, it should be remembered, was only John's pupil and one who craved affection, said to me: "Henry was not loved. He was a conscientious teacher, but rigid. He would not take a man's money for nothing: if a boy were sent to him, he could make him do all he could. No, he was not disagreeable. I learned to understand him later. I think that he was then in the green-apple stage."

Another scholar,[6] who was more with Henry, told a different story, remembering both brothers with great affection and gratitude. He said that after morning prayers, one or other of the brothers often made a little address to their scholars, original and interesting, to put their minds in proper train for the day's work. Henry's talks especially remain with him: on the seasons, their cause, their advantages, their adaptation to needs of organic life; their beauty, which he brought actually into the school-room by his description; on design in the universe, strikingly illustrated for children's minds; on profanity, treated in a way, fresh, amusing, and sensible.[7] At these times you could have heard a pin drop in the school-room. More than this, he won their respect. Such methods seem natural enough now, but were quite novel in those days.

Another[8] says: "What impressed me, then and later, was Henry's knowledge of Natural History; a keen observer and great student of things, and a very pleasant talker. He reminded me more of Gilbert White[†] of Selborne than any other character."

These brothers were just enough unlike to increase the interest and happiness of their relation. It was one of closest sympathy. It is believed that they were both charmed by one young girl: but she was denied them and passed out of their horizon. In reading what Thoreau says of Love and the two poems relating to his loss one sees that even his disappointment elevated his life.

The first of these is called "Sympathy,"[9] in which the lady is disguised as "a gentle boy." I give verses of the other below.

To the Maiden in the East

Low in the eastern sky
Is set thy glancing eye;
And though its gracious light
Ne'er riseth to my sight,
Yet every star that climbs
Above the gnarlèd limbs
       Of yonder hill
Conveys thy gentle will.

Believe I knew thy thought;
And that the zephyrs brought
Thy kindest wishes through,

---

†English clergyman and naturalist (1720–1793).

As mine they bear to you;
That some attentive cloud
Did pause amid the crowd
    Over my head,
While gentle things were said.

Believe the thrushes sung,
And that the flower-bells rung,
That herbs exhaled their scent
And hearts knew what was meant,
The trees a welcome waved,
And lakes the margins laved,
    When thy free mind
To my retreat did wind

Still will I strive to be
As if thou wert with me;
Whatever path I take
It shall be, for thy sake,
Of gentle slope and wide
As thou wert by my side.

During the summer vacation of their school the brothers made together that happy voyage, since famous, on the Rivers, but it was not in their dreams how soon Death, coming suddenly and in strange form, was to sunder their earthly lives. John, in full tide of happy life, died in a few days of lock-jaw following a most trifling cut. The shock, the loss, and the sight of his brother's terrible suffering at the end, for a time overthrew Henry so utterly that a friend told me he sat still in the house, could do nothing, and his sisters led him out passive to try to help him.

Near the same time died suddenly a beautiful child, with whom he had played and talked almost daily, in the house of near friends where he had a second home.[10]

He had gone into a Valley of Sorrow, but when, first, the dream of helpmate and guiding presence passed away, and then his nearest companion was taken from him, who shall say but that the presence of these blessings would have prevented his accomplishing his strange destiny? For his genius was solitary, and though his need for friendly and social relation with his kind was great, it was occasional, and to his lonely happiness the world will owe the best gifts he has left. And even as these his most prized and his coveted ties were parting or becoming impossible, new ones, more helpful if less desired, were presenting.

It is hard to name another town in Middlesex where the prevailing influences would have given the same push to the growth of his strong and original character as did those which were then in Concord. For from various causes, there early came that awakening of thought and spirit soon to spread wide in New England, then lethargic in physical prosperity, formal and sleepy in religion, selfish in politics, and provincial in its literature. At this period the young Thoreau came into constant contact with many persons resident or visiting there, full of the courage, the happiness, and the hope given by thoughts of a freer, nobler relation to God, and simpler and more humane ones to man. But be it distinctly understood that Thoreau was not created by the Transcendental Epoch, so-called, though, without doubt, his growth was stimulated by kindred ideas. His thoughtfulness in childhood, his independent course in college themes and early journals, prove that Thoreau was Thoreau and not the copy of another. His close association, under the same roof, for months, with the maturer Emerson[†] may, not unnaturally, have tinged his early writings, and some superficial trick of manner or of speech been unconsciously acquired, as often happens. But this is all that can be granted. Entire independence, strong individuality were Thoreau's distinguishing traits, and his foible was not subserviency, but combativeness in conversation, as his friends knew almost too well. Conscious imitation is not to be thought of as a possibility of this strong spirit.

Henry bravely recovered himself from the blow his brother's loss had been at first, when those who knew him said it seemed as if a part of himself had been torn away. Music seems to have been the first consoling voice that came to him, though great repairing Nature had silently begun to heal her son. He was

---

[†]Ralph Waldo Emerson (1803–82), father of the author of this book.

thrown more upon himself than before, and then he went out to her. Yet he cherished his friends, as his fine letters at this time show. In the next few years he worked with his father in the pencil shop (where now the Concord Library stands), and wrote constantly, and the woods and river drew him to them in each spare hour. He wrote for the *Dial*[†] as the organ of the new thought of the region and hour, though it paid nothing for articles, and he generously helped edit it. He relieved his friend Emerson from tasks hopeless to him by his skill in gardening and general household works, and went for a time to Staten Island as a private tutor to the son of Emerson's older brother, William.[11] In this visit to New York he became acquainted with Horace Greeley,[††] who appreciated his work and showed himself always generous and helpful in bringing it to publication in various magazines, and getting him paid for it.

Of Henry Thoreau as a mechanic thus much is known: that he helped his father more or less in his business of making lead-pencils; was instrumental in getting a better pencil than had been made up to that time in this country, which received a prize at the Mechanics' Fair; and that, when this triumph had been achieved, he promptly dropped the business which promised a good maintenance to himself and family: which unusual proceeding was counted to him for righteousness by a very few, and for laziness by most.

This is the principal charge made against him in his own neighbourhood. Many solid practical citizens, whose love of wild Nature was about like Dr. Johnson's,[†††] asserted that he neglected a good business, which he might have worked with profit for his family and himself, to idle in the woods, and this cannot be forgiven.

From my relation to the Thoreau family I knew something of their black-lead business after Henry's death, while carried on

---

[†]The magazine of the Transcendentalist literary movement, first published in July 1840.

[††]Born in 1811, he founded the *New York Tribune* in 1841 and edited it until his death in 1872.

[†††]Dr. Samuel Johnson (1709–84), English poet, essayist, and lexicographer.

by his sister, and later investigated the matter with some care and with results that are surprising. I will tell the story briefly.

John Thoreau, senior, went into the pencil business on his return to Concord in 1823. He made at first such bad pencils as were then made in America, greasy, gritty, brittle, inefficient, but tried to improve them, and did so. Henry found in the College library, in an encyclopædia published in Edinburgh, what the graphite ("black lead") was mixed with in the good German pencils, viz., a certain fine Bavarian clay; while here, glue, with a little spermaceti,[†] or bayberry wax, was used. The Thoreaus procured that clay, stamped with a crown as a royal monopoly, and baked it with the lead, and thus got a harder, blacker pencil than any here, but gritty. Then it appears they invented a process, very simple, but which at once put their black lead for fineness at the head of all manufactured in America. This was simply to have the narrow churn-like chamber around the mill-stones prolonged some seven feet high, opening into a broad, close, flat box, a sort of shelf. Only lead-dust that was fine enough to rise to that height, carried by an upward draught of air, and lodge in the box was used, and the rest ground over. I talked with the mechanic who showed me this, and who worked with the Thoreaus from the first, was actively helpful in the improvements and at last bought out the business from Mrs. Thoreau and carried it on for years,—and with others who knew something of the matter. The evidence is strong that Henry's mind and hand were active in the rapid carrying of this humble business to the front. It seems to be probable that, whether the father thought out the plan alone or with Henry, it was the latter's mechanical skill that put it into working shape. Henry is said also to have made the machine used in making their last and best pencil, which drilled a round hole into a solid wood and cut lead to fit it, as an axle does a wheel-box, instead of the usual method of having the wood in two parts glued together after filling.[12]

A friend who attended, in 1849, a fashionable school in

[†]A waxy substance obtained from the oil of sperm whales and other cetaceans.

Boston, kept by an English lady, tells me that the drawing-teacher used to direct the pupils to "ask at the art store for a *Thoreau pencil,* for they are the best"; for them they then had to pay a quarter of a dollar apiece. Henry Thoreau said of the best pencil when it was achieved, that it could not compete with the Fabers' because it cost more to make. They received, I am told, six dollars a gross for good pencils.[13]

But there is another chapter to the black-lead story not so well known. About 1848–49 the process of electrotyping was invented, it is claimed, in Boston. It was a secret process, and a man engaged in it, knowing the Thoreau lead was the best, ordered it in quantity from Mr. John Thoreau, the latter guarding carefully the secret of his method, and the former concealing the purpose for which he used it. Mr. Thoreau, senior, therefore increased his business and received good prices, at first ten dollars a pound,—though later it gradually fell to two dollars,—and sometimes selling five hundred pounds a year. After a time the purpose for which their lead was bought was found out by the Thoreaus and they sold it to various firms until after the death of Mr. John Thoreau and his son Henry, when the business was sold by Mrs. Thoreau.

Now, when Henry Thoreau succeeded in making his best pencil and deliberately renounced his partnership, saying that he could not improve on that product, and that his life was too valuable to him to put what remained of it into pencils, the principal trade of the family was in lead to the electrotypers, and after 1852 few pencils were made, and then merely to cover up the more profitable business, for, if the secret were known, it might be destroyed.

As his father became feebler Henry had to look after the business to some degree for the family, and to give some help after his father's death, though Miss Sophia attended to the correspondence, accounts, and directing and shipping the lead (brought in bulk, after grinding, to the house, that its destination might not be known) to the customers in Boston and New York. Yet Henry had to oversee the mill, bring the lead down, and help at the heavier part of boxing and packing, and this I am assured by two friends he did until his fatal sickness. The work was done in an upstairs room in the L, but the impalpable powder so pervaded the house, owing to the perfection of its reduction, that a friend tells me that, on opening Miss Sophia's piano, he found the keys coated with it. Thoreau's exposure to the elements and spare diet have been charged with shortening his life. He would probably much earlier have succumbed to a disease, hereditary in his family, had he held more closely to his trade with its irritant dust. The part he was obliged to bear in it certainly rendered him more susceptible to pulmonary disease, which his out-of-door life delayed.

Thus it appears that this ne'er-do-well worked at, and by his reading and thought and skill so helped on the improvements in the family's business, that they were far in advance of their competitors, and then, though he did not care to put his life into that trade, preferring trade with the Celestial City, yet found time quietly to oversee for the family the business which gave them a very good maintenance, and, when it was necessary, to work at it with his hands while health remained.

Yet he did not think fit to button-hole his neighbours on the street and say, "You mistake, Sir; I am not idle."

His own Spartan wants of plain food, strong clothing, and telescope, and a few books, with occasional travel in the cheapest way, were supplied in a variety of other ways. For he had what is called in New England, "faculty"; was a good gardener, mechanic, and emergency-man. He could do all sorts of jobbing and tinkering well at home and for other people. One or two fences were standing until lately, in town, which he built; he planted for his friend Emerson his barren pasture by Walden with pines. He especially loved to raise melons. I once went to a melon-party at his mother's with various people, young and old, where his work had furnished the handsome and fragrant pink or salmon fruit on which alone we were regaled; and he, the gardener, came in to help entertain the guests.

He wrote articles for magazines which brought him some money, and books, now classics, but hardly saleable in his day.

But his leading profession was that of a land-surveyor. In this, as in his mechanics, he did the best possible work. I remember his showing me some brass instrument which he had made or improved, with his own hands. Those who assisted him tell me that he was exceedingly particular, took more offsets than any other surveyor in these parts, often rectified bounds carelessly placed before. It amused him to call his friend Emerson from his study to ask him why he would steal his neighbour's meadow, showing him his hedge and ditch well inside the land that his good-natured neighbour, Sam Staples, had just bought and was entitled to by his deed, though the latter said, "No matter, let the ditch be the line," and would take no money.

Our leading surveyor, following Thoreau, told me that he soon learned by running over again Thoreau's lines that he was sure to find his plans minutely accurate if he made in them correction required by the variation of the compass, some degrees since Thoreau's day. Never but once did he find an error, and that was not in angular measurement and direction, but in distance, one chain, probably an error in count of his assistant. Thoreau did work in the spirit of George Herbert's[†] prayer two hundred years before:—

> "Teach me, my God, my King,
>   In all things Thee to see,
> And what I do in any thing
>   To do it as for Thee.

> "Not rudely as a beast
>   To run into an action,
> But still to make Thee prepossessed
>   And give it its perfection."

He wrote: "I would not be one of those who will foolishly drive a nail into mere lath and plastering: such a deed would keep me awake nights. Give me a hammer and let me feel for the furring. Drive a nail home, and clinch it so faithfully, that you can wake up in the night and think of your work with satisfaction, a work at which you would not be ashamed to invoke the Muse. So will help you God, and so only. Every nail driven

---

†Welsh metaphysical poet (1593–1633).

should be as another rivet in the machine of the universe, you carrying on the work." Small things for him symbolized great.

Thoreau enjoyed his surveying, and the more if it led him into the wild lands *East of the Sun, West of the Moon.* But he construed his business largely, looking deeper than its surface. While searching for their bounds with his townsmen and neighbours in village, swamp, and woodlot, he found everywhere, marked far more distinctly than by blazed black-oak tree or stake and stones, lines, imaginary truly, but forming bounds to their lives more impassable than stone. Many he saw imprisoned for life, and he found these walls already beginning to hedge in his horizon, shut out the beautiful free life of his hope, and saw that, in the end, the converging walls might even shut out the blessed Heaven. What if the foundations of these walls were justice, natural right, human responsibility; and the first tier of blocks of experience, goodwill, and reverence, if the upper stories were fashion, conservatism, unenlightened public opinion, party politics, dishonest usage of trade, immoral law, and the arch and key-stones the dogmas still nominally accepted by Christian Congregational churches in the first half of the nineteenth century? Who would take a vault with the Last Judgment frescoed on it, even by Michael Angelo, in exchange for Heaven's blue cope, painted by the oldest Master with cloud and rainbow, and jewelled by night with his worlds and suns?

> "Heaven lies about us in our infancy,"

sang the poet, and Thoreau, mainly to save a view of those heavens, and, that the household clatter and village hum drown not the music of the spheres, went into the woods for a time.

His lifelong friend, Mr. Harrison G. O. Blake, of Worcester, pointed out that Thoreau, feeling that the best institutions, home, school, public organization, were aimed to help the man or woman to lead a worthy life—"instead of giving himself to some profession or business, whereby he might earn those superfluities which men have agreed to call a living; instead of thus earning a position in society and so acting upon it; instead of trying to see how the town, the State, the Country might be better governed, so that future generations might come nearer to the ideal life, he proposed to lead that life at once himself, as far as possible." To this cause "he early turned with simplicity and directness."[14]

When the spirit clearly shows a man of high purpose what his gift is, or may be, his neighbours must not insist on harnessing him into a team,—just one more to pull through their crude or experimental reform,—or require of him exact following of village ways or city fashion. We all know persons whose quiet light shining apart from public action has more illuminated and guided our lives.

As a man who once had some knowledge of the habits of our people, such as a country doctor acquires, I may say that I found that the root of much disease, disappointment, and blight was, that few persons stand off and look at the way their days pass, but live minute by minute, and as is customary, and therefore never find that the day, the year, and the lifetime pass in preparation to live, but the time to live never comes—here, at least. Thoreau couldn't do this, for he was a surveyor—one who oversees the ground, and takes account of direction and distance. Be sure his life at Walden was an experiment in keeping means and ends in their proper relative positions. He was not one who lived to eat.

Speaking of what his solitary and distant wood-walks were worth to him, he writes in his journal: "I do not go there to get my dinner, but to get that sustenance which dinners only preserve me to enjoy, without which dinners were a vain repetition." "We dine," he said, "at the sign of the shrub-oak."

"If I should sell both my forenoons and afternoons to society," wrote Thoreau in his journal, "as most appear to do, I am sure that for me there would be nothing left worth living for. I trust that I shall never thus sell my birthright for a mess of pottage. I wish to suggest that a man may be very industrious, and yet not spend his time well. There is no more fatal blunderer than he who consumes the greater part of his life getting his living. All great enterprises are self-supporting. The poet, for instance, must sustain his body by his poetry, as a steam planing-mill feeds its boilers with the shavings it makes. You must get your living by loving."

Mr. Emerson noted in his journal, a few years before this

Walden venture: "Henry made last night the fine remark that 'as long as a man stands in his own way, everything seems to be in his way,—governments, society, and even the sun and moon and stars, as astrology may testify.'" Now he put aside doubt and custom, and all went well.

In these changed days, when the shores of our beautiful pond have been devastated by fire and moths and rude and reckless visitors, when the white sand and whiter stony margin of the cove have been defiled by coke cinders, when even the clear waters have ebbed, it is pleasant to turn to the picture of what Thoreau looked out on seventy years ago: "When I first paddled a boat on Walden it was completely surrounded by thick and lofty pine and oak woods and in some of its coves grapevines had run over the trees next the water and formed bowers under which a boat could pass. The hills which form its shores were so steep, and the woods on them were then so high, that, as you looked down from the west end, it had the appearance of an amphitheatre for some kind of sylvan spectacle."

His sojourn in Walden woods, as seen by his townsmen, told by himself, and rumoured abroad, made a stronger impression, and more obvious, than any part of his strong and original life. He is more thought of as a hermit, preaching by life and word a breach with society, than in any other way; and this notion is so widespread that it seems to require a few words here.

And, first, it must be remembered that the part of his life lived in the Walden house was from July 4, 1845, to September 6, 1847, just two years and two months of his forty-four years of life. They were happy, wholesome years, helping his whole future by their teachings. He did not go there as a Jonah crying out on Nineveh, but simply for his own purposes, to get advantageous conditions to do his work, exactly as a lawyer or banker or any man whose work requires concentration is sure to leave his home to do it. He prepared there his first and perhaps best book, the "Week on the Concord and Merrimac Rivers," for publication; he tried his spiritual, intellectual, social and economic experiment, and recorded it; and incidentally made an interesting survey and history of one of the most beautiful and remarkable ponds in Massachusetts. Meantime he earned the few dollars that it took to keep him.

Unlike the prophet at Nineveh, he went to the woods to mind his own business in the strictest sense, and there found the freedom, joy, and blessed influences that came of so simple and harmless a life, nearer the flowers and stars, and the God that the child had looked for behind the stars, free from the mill-stones, even the carved and gilded ones, which customary town life hangs around the necks of most of us. Then, when he went down into the village, found the good people set at such elementary problems as they seem to us now, and then to him,—whether it was right for this country to uphold human slavery, or for man to withhold from woman her right in her property, or for persons to get somewhat drunk frequently, or for a citizen to violate a law requiring him to become a slave hunter, or whether an innocent, blameless person dying, not a church member, had any chance of escaping the terrible wrath, not of the Adversary, but of his Maker, which should be exercised on him for untold millions of years,—or perhaps found advanced philosophers spending their time discussing if more aspiration cannot come from eating upward-growing vegetables like wheat, instead of burrowing, darkling carrots or grovelling turnips; or the soul may not be polluted by eating "raised bread"; or again, when he found the people spending their rare holidays in the bar-room, or the old-time muster-field, strewn with fired ramrods, and redolent of New England rum and bad language and worse discipline, or, having forced their farm-work that they might do so, spending days listening to the foul or degrading details of the Criminal Court session, or cheering blindly for Webster[†] after his deliberate desertion of all that he had once stood for to best New England,—no wonder, then, I say, that he rejoiced that his neck was out of such yokes, and his eyes washed clearer by Walden water, and, as his generous instinct always bade him share the knowledge he won, he

> "Chanted the bliss of his abode,
>   To men imprisoned in their own."

[†]Daniel Webster (1782–1852), U.S. Senator and famed orator who, as Secretary of State, insisted on enforcement of the Fugitive Slave Act.

By village firesides on winter evenings his foolish whim was gossiped over with pity; but the wind harping gloriously in the pine boughs over his hut, as he sat at his Spartan feast below, sang to him like the Sea-King, whose

> "hands that loved the oar,
> Now dealt with the rippling harp-gold, and he
>   sang of the shaping of earth,
> And how the stars were lighted, and where the
>   winds had birth;
> And the gleam of the first of summers on the
>   yet untrodden grass.
> What though above the roof-tree they heard
>   the thunder pass,
> Yet had they tales for song-craft and the
>   blossoming garth of rhyme,
> Tales of the framing of all things, and the
>   entering in of Time
> From the halls of the outer heaven, so near
>   they knew the door."

Hear his story of his high company:—

"I have occasional visits in the long winter evenings, when the snow falls fast and the wind howls in the woods, from an old settler and original proprietor, who is reported to have dug Walden Pond and stoned it around, and fringed it with pine woods; who tells me stories of old time and new eternity; and between us we manage to pass a cheerful evening with social mirth and pleasant views of things, even without apples and cider,—a most wise and humorous friend, whom I love much, who keeps himself more secret than ever did Goffe or Whalley;[15] and though he is thought to be dead, none can show where he is buried. An elderly dame, too, dwells in my neighbourhood, invisible to most persons, in whose odorous herb-garden I love to stroll sometimes, gathering simples and listening to her fables; for she has a genius of unequalled fertility, and her memory runs back farther than mythology, and she can tell me the original of every fable, and on what fact every one is founded, for the incidents occurred when she was young. A ruddy and lusty old dame, who delights in all weathers and seasons, and is likely to outlive all her children yet."

Again he wrote: "I silently smiled at my incessant good fortune."

They err entirely who suppose that he counselled every one to build hermitages in the woods, break with society and live on meal. This he distinctly disavows, but makes a plea for simple and brave living, not drowned in the details, not merely of cooking, sweeping, and dusting, but of politics, whether parish, town, state, or federal, and even of societies, religious, professional, charitable, or social, for, after all, these are but preparatory,—police regulations on a larger or smaller scale,—designed as means to make life possible, and not to be pursued as ends. Even by Walden, as he tells us, he wore a path, and he found that his life there was falling into it: evidently he saw it was incomplete, so, keeping its sweet kernel, he left the shell. In cheerful mood, years after, he discusses the matter: "Why did I change? Why did I leave the woods? I do not think that I can tell. I have often wished myself back. I do not know any better how I came to go there. Perhaps it is none of my business, even if it is yours. Perhaps I wanted change. There was a little stagnation, it may be, about 2 o'clock in the afternoon. Perhaps if I lived there much longer, I might live there forever. One would think twice before he accepted Heaven on such terms."

Taking a bird's-eye view of institutions and marking their provisional and makeshift and hence transitory character, he writes in his journal: "As for dispute about solitude and society, any comparison is impertinent. It is an idling down on a plain at the base of a mountain instead of climbing steadily to its top. Of course, you will be glad of all the society you can get to go up with. 'Will you go to Glory with me?' is the burden of the song. It is not that we love to be alone, but that we love to soar, and, when we do soar, the company grows thinner and thinner, till there is none at all. It is either the *Tribune* or the plain, a sermon on the Mount, or a very private ecstasy higher up. Use all the society that will abet you."

And now as to the belief that he was hard, stern, selfish, or misanthropic. Truly he was undemonstrative; a sisterly friend said of him, "As for taking his arm, I should as soon think of taking the arm of an elm-tree as Henry's"; and he, himself, said, "When I am dead you will find swamp-oak written on my heart";

but under this oak-bark was friendship and loyalty in the tough grain, through and through. He was a friend, "even to the altars," too sincere and true to stoop to weakness from his noble ideal. Hear his creed of sincere yet austere friendship as he states it in his journal:—

"It steads us to be as true to children and boors as to God himself. It is the only attitude which will suit all occasions, it only will make the Earth yield her increase, and by it do we effectually expostulate with the wind. If I run against a post, *that* is the remedy. I would meet the morning and evening on very sincere grounds. When the sun introduces me to a new day, I silently say to myself, 'Let us be faithful all round. We will do justice and receive it.' Something like this is the charm of Nature's demeanour towards us; strict conscientiousness and disregard of us when we have ceased to have regard to ourselves. So she can never offend us. How true she is, and never swerves. In her most genial moment her laws are as steadfastly and relentlessly fulfilled—though the Decalogue is rhymed and set to sweetest music—as in her sternest. Any exhibition of affection, as an inadvertent word, or act or look, seems premature, as if the time were not ripe for it, like the buds which the warm days near the end of winter cause to push out and unfold before the frosts are yet gone."

Again he writes that in the relation of friends: "There is no ambition except virtue, for why should we go round about who may go direct? All those contingencies which the philanthropist, statesman, and housekeeper write so many books to meet are simply and quietly settled in the intercourse of friends."

I can bring my own witness and that of many others to his quiet, dutiful, loyal attitude to his mother and father, how respectfully he listened to them, whether he agreed with them or not; how in his quiet way he rendered all sorts of useful and skillful help in domestic and household matters. After his father's death his mother said, "But for this I should never have seen the tender side of Henry," who had nursed him with loving care. His family were a little anxious and troubled when he went to Walden, fearing danger and hardship in this life, and they missed him; but they sympathized with his desire and wanted him to carry it out as pleased him. He came constantly home to see them and to help them in garden or house, and also dropped in at other friendly homes in the village, where he was always welcome at table or fireside.

The mighty indictment that he was not honest in his experiment, for he did not live exclusively on his own meal and rice, but often accepted one of his mother's pies, or chanced in at a friend's at supper-time, seems too frivolous to notice, but since it is so often made, I will say that Henry Thoreau, while he could have lived uncomplainingly where an Esquimau could, on *tripe de roche* lichen and blubber, if need were (for never was man less the slave of appetite and luxury), was not a prig, nor a man of so small pattern as to be tied to a rule-of-thumb in diet, and ungraciously thrust back on his loving mother her gift. Nor was there the slightest reason that he should forego his long-established habit of appearing from time to time at nightfall, a welcome guest at the fireside of friends. He came for friendship, not for food. "I was never so effectually deterred from frequenting a man's house by any kind of Cerberus whatever," he says, "as by the parade one made about dining me, which I took to be a very polite and roundabout hint never to trouble him so again." And, fully to satisfy cavil, it is certain that he overpaid his keep in mere handiwork, which he convinced all friends that it was a favour to him to allow him to do for them (such as burning out chimneys, setting stoves, door-knobs, or shutters to right), to make no mention of higher service.

He was not a professing philanthropist, though steadily friendly to his kind as he met them. His eminent, but unappreciative, critic, Lowell,[†] said severely, among other charges, "Did his plan of life seem selfish—he condemned doing good as one of the weakest of superstitions." Here is Thoreau's word seventy-five years ago. Possibly it may commend itself to some good people who have large experience of the results of alms-giving: "There are a thousand hacking at the branches of evil to one who is striking at the root, and it may be that he who bestows the

---

†James Russell Lowell.

largest amount of time and money on the needy is doing the most by his mode of life to produce that misery which he strives in vain to relieve."

I cannot quite omit the discussion of his refusal to pay his poll-tax when the slave power had forced on the country a war of invasion of Mexico,† and his consequent imprisonment in Concord jail. Ordinarily a good citizen, he held then that good government had sunk so low that his time to exercise the reserve right of revolution had come. He made no noise, but quietly said to the State, through its official, "No, I wash my hands of you, and won't contribute my mite to your wrong-doing." What if nine tenths of the money were well spent; he felt it was the only chance of protest a citizen had thus to show his disapproval of the low public measures of the day. It was the act of a poet rather than a logician—symbolic—but read his paper on "Civil Disobedience," and, whatever one thinks of the conclusion, one must respect the man. I must not fail to record the pleasant circumstance that the tax collector, good Sam Staples, also constable and jailor, before arresting him said, "I'll pay your tax, Henry, if you're hard up," not understanding, as he found by Henry's refusal, and, later, by Mr. Alcott's,†† that "'T was nothin' but principle." He always liked and respected Thoreau, but when he told me the story, he added, "I wouldn't have done it for old man Alcott." He knew a good fellow and surveyor, but did not prize a Platonist.[16]

His short imprisonment was a slight enough matter to Thoreau. He mentions his night spent there in "Walden," in an entertaining line or two. An incident, not there told, I learned from a friend. He was kept awake by a man in the cell below ejaculating, "What is life?" and, "So this is life!" with a painful monotony. At last, willing to get whatever treasure of truth this sonorous earthen vessel might hold, Thoreau put his head to the iron window-bars and asked suddenly, "Well, What *is* life,

†The Mexican War, 1846–48, initiated by Pres. James F. Polk.
††(Amos) Bronson Alcott (1799–1888), Neo-Platonist educator and Transcendentalist philosopher; father of Louisa May Alcott.

then?" but got no other reward than the sleep of the just, which his fellow-martyr did not further molest.

After dark, some person, unrecognized by Staples's little daughter, who went to the door, left with the child some money "to pay Mr. Thoreau's tax." Her father came home too late to hear of it, but in the morning gladly sent Thoreau away.[17]

To the criticism, Why did he allow his tax to be paid? the simple answer is, He couldn't help it, and did not know who did it. Why, then, did he go out of jail? Because they would not keep him there.[18]

But in a few more years the Slavery question began to darken the day. Many good men woke in the morning to find themselves sick at heart because we were becoming a slave country. The aggressive tone of the South increased, and with it the subserviency of a large class of Northern business men and manufacturers of cotton cloth, who feared to offend the planters. John Randolph's† hot words in the debate over the Missouri Compromise were recalled as too nearly true: "We do not govern the people of the North by our black slaves, but by their own white slaves. We know what we are doing. We have conquered you once, and we can and will conquer you again." The idolized Webster turned recreant and countenanced a law punishing with imprisonment and heavy fine any person who should shelter, hide, or help any alleged black fugitive. Of this law our honoured Judge Hoar said in Court from the bench, "If I were giving my private opinion I might say, that statute seems to me to evince a more deliberate and settled disregard of all principles of constitutional liberty than any other enactment that has ever come under my notice.[19]

This question of Slavery came to Thoreau's cabin door. He did not seek it. He solved it as every true man must when the moment comes to choose whether he will obey the law, or do right. He sheltered the slave and helped and guided him, and

---

†U.S. Senator and Representative from Virginia (1773–1833), active at the time of the Missouri Compromise (1820).

others, later, on their way towards the North Star and the rights of a man.

After Stevenson[†] had published in his "Men and Books" his views of Thoreau, whom, of course, he had never seen,[20] saying, that in his whole works there is no trace of pity, Mr. Alexander H. Japp contributed this true story of the effective tenderness of the man. It was told by Moncure D. Conway, the brave young Virginian preacher, who had left his home and forgone his inheritance of slaves for conscience' sake. He lived for a time in Concord, near the Thoreaus, when a hunted slave came to the village by night to the home of that family.

"When I went [there] next morning, I found them all in a state of excitement by reason of the arrival of a fugitive negro from the South, who had come fainting to their door about day-break and thrown himself upon their mercy. Thoreau took me in to see the poor wretch, whom I found to be a man with whose face, as that of a slave from the South, I was familiar. The negro was much terrified at seeing me, supposing I was one of his pur-suers. Having quieted his fears by the assurance that I, too, but in a different sense, was a refugee from the bondage he was escaping, and at the same time being able to attest the negro's genuineness, I sat and watched the singularly tender and lowly devotion of the scholar to the slave. He must be fed, his swollen feet bathed, and he must think of nothing but rest: again and again this coolest and calmest of men drew near to the trem-bling negro, and soothed him and bade him feel at home, and have no fear that any power should again wrong him. Thoreau could not walk with me that day, as had been agreed, but must mount guard over the fugitive, for slave-hunters were not extinct in those days, and so I went away, after a while, much impressed by many little traits that I had seen as they appeared in this emergency."

Thoreau by no means neglected all civic duties. The low moral tone of his country stirred him, so that again and again he left

---

†Robert Louis Stevenson (1850–94), versatile English writer best known for his adventure novels.

the quiet, consoling woods and meadows to speak in Concord and elsewhere for freedom of person, of thought, and of conscience. He gave the countenance of his presence and speech to the meetings for the relief and self-protection against murder and outrage of the Free State settlers in Kansas, and contributed money. He admired John Brown, the sturdy farmer with whom he had talked on his visits to Concord, as a liberator of men, and one who dared to defend the settlers' rights. But, later, when two successive administrations ignored the outrages, and steadily favoured the party which were committing them, Thoreau, hopeless of any good coming of the United States Government, thoroughly sympathized with a man who had courage to break its bonds in the cause of natural right. In the first days of the Harper's Ferry raid, when Brown's friends and backers, hitherto, were in doubt as to their attitude in this crisis, Thoreau, taking counsel of none, announced that he should speak in the church vestry, on John Brown, to whoever came. It was as if he spoke for his own brother, so deeply stirred was he, so searching and brave his speech. Agree or disagree,—all were moved. "Such a man as it takes ages to make, and ages to under-stand; . . . sent to be a redeemer of those in captivity;—and the only use to which you can put him is to hang him at the end of a rope!"

For Thoreau prized moral courage. He once wrote: "Nothing is so much to be feared as fear. The sin that God hates is fear: he thinks Atheism innocent in comparison."[21]

Thoreau was a good talker, but a certain enjoyment in taking the other side for the joy of intellectual fencing, and a pleasure of startling his companions by a paradoxical statement of his highly original way of looking at things, sometimes, were baf-fling to his friends. His ancestry on his mother's side, the Dunbars, was Scotch, and he had the national instinct of dispu-tation, pugnacity, love of paradoxical statement. This fatal ten-dency to parry and hit with the tongue, as his ancestors no doubt did with cudgel or broadsword, for no object but the fun of intellectual fence, as such, was a temperamental fault standing in the way of relations that would otherwise have been perfect with his friends. One could sometimes only think of his Uncle

Charles Dunbar, once well known in the neighbourhood for his friendly desire to "burst" his acquaintances in wrestling. Thoreau held this trait in check with women and children, and with humble people who were no match for him. With them he was simple, gentle, friendly, and amusing;[22] and all testify his desire to share all the pleasant things he learned in his excursions. But to a conceited gentleman from the city, or a dogmatic or patronizing clergyman or editor, he would, as Emerson said, appear as a "gendarme, good to knock down cockneys with and go on his way smiling." His friend Channing[†] says: "Though nothing was less to his mind than chopped logic, he was ready to accommodate those who differed from him with his opinion and never too much convinced by opposition."

He could afford to be a philosopher, for he was first a good common man. It takes good iron to receive a fine polish. His simple, direct speech and look and bearing were such that no plain, common man would put him down in his books as a fool, or visionary, or helpless, as the scholar, writer, or reformer would often be regarded by him. Much of Alcibiades's description of Socrates in Plato's "Symposium" would apply to Thoreau. He loved to talk with all kinds and conditions of men if they had no hypocrisy or pretence about them, and though high in his standard of virtue, and most severe with himself, could be charitable to the failings of humble fellow-men.[23] His interest in the Indian was partly one of natural history, and the human interest was because of the genuineness of the Indian's knowledge and his freedom from cant.

There was then a genus of man (now nearly extinct) well known along the Musketaquid, amphibious, weather-beaten, solitary, who though they had homes, and even kin in some remote little farmhouse, where at odd times they hoed corn and beans, yet spent the best of their lives floating in a flat skiff, which they mainly poled along the banks, and silent, consoled by Nature and by rum, passed their best days getting fish from the river, which in the end absorbed them, even as the beautiful

---

†William Ellery Channing (1818–1901), poet and journalist.

Hylas was taken down, sleeping, by the nymphs to the dreamy ooze; and thus what was fitting happened, and the fishes had their turn. I cannot forego giving what some will recognize as a true picture of them by another hand:[24]

"Among the blue-flowered pickerel-weed
In grey old skiff that nestles low
Half hid in shining arrow-leaves,
The fisher sits,—nor heeds the show.
His rounded back, all weather-stained,
Has caught the air of wave-worn rocks,
And sun and wind have bleached and tanned
To one dun hue, hat, face, and locks.
And Nature's calm so settled there
The fishes never know their danger
And playful take his careless bait—
Bait they would ne'er accept from stranger.
The blue eyes only are shrewd and living,
But of soft reflections and fair things seen
To you and me no hint they are giving—
Of Sunsets' splendor, or meadows green,
Never they prate of the cardinal's flame,
The lilies' freshness, and sunrise flush,
The solemn night, or the morning star,
The violets white and the wild rose flush.
Is it all a picture? Or does he ponder
The year's fair pageant he knows so well?
Or had it reached his heart, I wonder?
He and the rushes will never tell."

For these men Thoreau felt an especial attraction and, himself a good fisher, but in no cockney fashion, and able to startle them with secrets of their own craft, could win others from them.[25] From the most ancient of these it appears that he got that description of Walden in the last century given in his book, exciting to read in these sad days of "Lake Walden," a miscellaneous picnic ground.

One of the young men who helped him survey had pleasant recollection of his wealth of entertainment by instruction given afield, opening the way to studies of his own; and also of his good humour and fun. One who made collections for

Agassiz[†] and the Smithsonian was thus first led to natural history; but said that, were he in trouble and need of help, he thought he should as soon have turned to Henry Thoreau as any man in town. Another, born on a farm, who knew and had worked in the black-lead mill many years, said, when I asked what he thought of Thoreau: "Why, he was the best friend I ever had. He was always straight in his ways: and was very particular to make himself agreeable. Yes, he was always straight and true: you could depend upon him: all was satisfactory." Was he a kindly and helpful man? "Yes, he was all of that: what we call solid and true, but he couldn't bear any gouge-game and dishonesty. When I saw him crossing my field I always wanted to go and have a talk with him. He was more company for me than the general run of neighbours. I liked to hear his ideas and get information from him. He liked to talk as long as you did, and what he said was new; mostly about Nature. I think he went down to Walden to pry into the arts of Nature and get something that wasn't open to the public. He liked the creatures. He seemed to think their nature could be improved. Some people called him lazy: I didn't deem it so. I called him industrious, and he was a first-rate mechanic. He was a good neighbour and very entertaining. I found him a particular friend."

A lady in Indianapolis told me that President Jordan, of Leland Stanford University, California, told her that, when travelling in Wisconsin, some years since, he was driven by an Irish farmer, Barney Mullens, once of Concord. He asked him if he knew Thoreau. "Oh, yes," said Mullens. "He was a land surveyor. He had a way of his own, and didn't care naught about money, but if there was ever a gentleman alive he was one."

I had a pleasant talk with Mrs. Minot Pratt. She and her husband, who had been members of the Brook Farm Community,[††] in the failure of which they had lost almost all their property,

---

[†]Louis Agassiz (1807–73), Swiss-born naturalist who arrived in the United States in 1846 and was a professor at Harvard for 25 years.
[††]An experiment in agriculture and education (1841–47) founded by some members of the Transcendentalist movement.

settled in Concord on its dispersal. They early became acquainted with the Thoreaus. Mr. Pratt was a high-minded, kindly farmer, and a botanist. So common tastes soon made him a friend of Thoreau.

Mrs. Pratt said that he used to come much to their house. He was sociable and kind, and always seemed at home. They liked his ways, like their own, and believed in them; no pretence, no show; let guests and friends come at any time, and take them as they find them. "Henry lived in a lofty way. I loved to hear him talk, but I did not like his books so well, though I often read them and took what I liked. They do not do him justice. I liked to see Thoreau rather in his life. Yes, he was religious; he was more like the ministers than others; that is, like what they would wish and try to be. I loved him, but . . . always felt a little in awe of him.

"He loved to talk, like all his family, but not to gossip: he kept the talk on a high plane. He was cheerful and pleasant."

Just before Thoreau built his Walden house the Fitchburg Railroad was being laid through Concord, and a small army of Irishmen had their rough shanties in the woods along the deep cuts, and some of them, later good Concord citizens, had their wives and little children in these rude abodes; the remains of excavation and banking can still be traced near Walden. These people seemed a greater innovation than Samoans would to-day. Thoreau talked with them in his walks and took some kindly interest. I well remember the unusual wrath and indignation he felt a few years later when one of these, a poor neighbour, industrious but ignorant, had his spading-match prize at Cattle Show taken by his employer, on the plea, "Well, as I pay for his time, what he gets in the time I pay for nat'rally comes to me," and I know that Thoreau raised the money to make good the poor man's loss, and, I think, made the farmer's ears burn.

Once or twice I knew of the kindling of that anger, and reproof bravely given, as when an acquaintance, who had a faithful dog, discarded and drove him away out of caprice; and again, when a buyer of hens set a dog to catch them. His remarks in his book about the man getting faithful work out of the horse day by day, but doing nothing whatever to help the horse's condition, is suggestive reading for any horse-owner. He felt real respect for the personality and character of animals, and could never have been guilty of asking with Paul, "Doth God care for oxen?" The humble little neighbours in house or wood whose characters he thus respected, rewarded his regard by some measure of friendly confidence. He felt that until men showed higher behaviour, the less they said about the "lower animals" the better.

For all life he had reverence, and just where the limits of conscious life began and ended he was too wise, and too hopeful, to say.

Some naturalists of the Dry-as-dust School are critical of him because he was not, like them, a cataloguer, and mere student of dead plants and animals. I remember once hearing Virchow, the great authority on physiology and pathology in Berlin, laugh to scorn the study of dry bones, for he said they are artificial, have no existence in Nature. The student of bones must study fresh bones with the marrow in them, the ligaments and periosteum still attached, the blood in their vessels and canals, if he would know anything of nature. Thoreau considered that one living bird for study, in its proper haunts, was worth more than a sackful of bird-skins and skeletons. A brown, brittle plant in a portfolio gave him little comfort, but he knew the day in March when it would show signs of life, the days in August when it would be in flower, and what birds would come in January from far Labrador to winter on those particular seeds that its capsule held stored for them above the snow.

His friend Emerson writing to another, whom he hoped to lure to Concord said: "If old Pan were here, you would come: and we have young Pan here, under another name, whom you shall see, and hear his reeds, if you tarry not."

Surely a better mortal to represent what the Greek typified in his sylvan god we might search New England long to find. For years, a wanderer in the outskirts of our village was like to meet this sturdy figure striding silently through tangled wood or wild meadow at any hour of day or night; yet he would vent his happiness in a wild and gay dance, or yet again lie motionless in any weather in a lonely wood, waiting for his friends, the wild creatures, and winning in the match with them of leisure and patience. When at length the forest began to show its little heads, the utterance of a low, continuous humming sound, like those of Nature, spoke to their instincts and drew them to him. Like the wood-gods of all peoples, he guarded trees and flowers and springs, showed a brusque hospitality to mortals wandering in the wood, *so they violated not its sanctities;* and in him was the immortal quality of youth and cheerfulness.

Thoreau had the humour which often goes with humanity. It crops out slyly in all his writings, but sometimes is taken for dead earnest because the reader did not know the man.

He would say with a certain gravity, "It does no harm whatever to mowing to walk through it: but as it does harm to the owner's feelings, it is better not to do it when he is by." Read his very human yet humorous remarks upon his half-witted and his one-and-a-half-witted visitors at Walden, and on the "spirit knockings" in Concord,[26] and, in Mr. Channing's biography, his charming description of the drunken young Dutch deck-hand on the boat.

While living at Walden he wrote: "One evening I overtook one of my townsmen, who has accumulated what is called a handsome property,—through I never got a *fair* view of it,—on the Walden road, driving a pair of cattle to market, who inquired of me how I could bring my mind to give up so many of the comforts of life. I answered that I was very sure that I liked it passably well; I was not joking. And so I went home to my bed and left him to pick his way through the darkness and the mud to Brighton,—or Bright-town,—which place he would reach some time in the morning."

Thoreau said he once overheard one of his auditors at a country Lyceum after the lecture say to another, "What does he lecture for?"—a question which made him quake in his shoes.

I forget of what the following amusing uttterance is apropos: "If you are chosen Town Clerk, forsooth, you cannot go to Terra del Fuego[†] this summer: but you may go to the land of infernal fire nevertheless. The universe is wider than our views of it."

When, on occasion of some convention, some divines tarried

---

†Tierra del Fuego, "Fire Land," the southern tip of South America.

at his mother's, one of these persons told the aunts that he wished Henry would go and hear him, saying, "I have a sermon on purpose for him." The aunts gave little hope, but presently Henry came in and was introduced. Immediately this clergyman slapped him on the shoulder with his fat hand, exclaiming familiarly, "So here's the chap who camped in the woods." Thoreau turned round and said promptly, "And here's the chap that camps in a pulpit." His assailant was discomfited and said no more.

In the reed-pipes of Pan slept the notes of enchantment for him to wake at will. Our Concord genius of the wood was a master of the flute. It was his companion in his life there and the echoes of Walden hills were his accompaniments.[27]

Music was an early and life-long friend. His sisters made home pleasant with it. The sweet tunes of Mrs. Hawthorne's† music-box were a comfort to him in the lonely days after John's death. "Row, Brothers, Row," which I have heard him sing, recalled the happy river-voyage; and no one who heard "Tom Bowling" from Thoreau could ask if he were capable of human feeling. To this day that song, heard long years ago, rings clear and moving to me.

He studied the songs of birds as eagerly as many a man how to make money. Milton calls Mammon,—

> "The least erected spirit that fell
> From Heaven, for even in Heaven his looks and thoughts
> Were always downward bent, admiring more
> The riches of Heaven's pavement, trodden gold,
> Than aught divine or holy else enjoyed
> In vision beatific."

Not so Henry Thoreau. As he walked the village street sometimes it happened that his towns-folk were hurt or annoyed that his eyes were far away and he did not stop "to pass the time of day." There was no affectation or unkindness here. The real man was then in the elm-arch high aloft,—

---

†Sophie (Peabody) Hawthorne, wife of Nathaniel.

"The beautiful hanging gardens that rocked
    in the morning wind
And sheltered a dream of Faerie and a life so
    timid and kind,
The shady choir of the bluebird and the race-
    course of squirrels gay."

He stopped once on the street and made me hear, clear, but far above, the red-eyed vireo's note and, rarely coming, that of his little white-eyed cousin. I had not known—I venture to say few persons know—that the little olive-brown bird whom we associate with her delicate nest hanging between two twigs in the woods, is one of the commonest singers on our main street in July, even as Thoreau wrote:—

"Upon the lofty elm-tree sprays,
The Vireo rings the changes meet,
During these trivial summer days,
Striving to lift our thoughts above the street."

Many a boy and girl owed to him the opening of the gate of this almost fairy knowledge, and thereafter pleasant voices, unnoted of others, spoke to him, like the sudden understanding of the eagle's voices to Sigurd in the Saga.

He was more than Naturalist. He said of Nature, "She must not be looked at directly, but askance, or by flashes: like the head of the Gorgon Medusa, she turns the men of Science to stone." But the walls of Troy are said to have builded themselves of stone obedient to immortal music, and though those walls be crumbled, they endure in the song of the blind harper.

In the ages called dark, and what we think of as rude times, one wanderer was sure of welcome,—wherever he went was free of market and inn, of camp and castle and palace; he who could tell in song or story of the gods and the darker powers; the saints, the helping heroes, and gracious beauty. These men by their magic made hard life seem sweet, and bloody death desirable, and raised in each the hope that even the short thread of life spun out to him by grudging Fate might yet gleam in the glorious tapestry of story.

And the men and maids for one moment knew
That the song was truer than what was true.

Our hero was a born story-teller, and of the Norseman type in many ways, a right Saga-man and Scald like them, telling of woods and waters and the dwarfkin that peopled them—and ever he knew what he saw for a symbol, and looked through it for a truth. "Even the facts of science," said he, "may dust the mind by their dryness, unless they are in a sense effaced by the dews of fresh and living truth."

When one asked Aristotle, why we like to spend much time with handsome people? "That is a blind man's question," was the wise man's answer; and Thoreau, looking at beautiful Mother Nature, might have given the same answer to a townsman anxious lest he stay in the fields too long for the good of pencil-making. How Thoreau felt when alone with Nature may be gathered from his words about her, "At once our Destiny and Abode, our Maker and our Life."

The humour, the raciness, and the flavour of the moor and the greenwood that is in the Robin Hood ballads he loved, was in his speech. In his books, particularly "Walden," the contentious tone may linger unpleasantly in the reader's ears and memory, but remember, Thoreau, in his day, was administering wholesome, if bitter, medicine. Yet when he at last lays by his wholesome but fatiguing buffeting North-wind method, there comes winning sunshine; and the enchanting haze of a poet's thought brings out the true beauty in the commonest things.

Some of his verses are little better than doggerel, but others, hardly yet received, will, I think, remain when many who passed current as American poets, in his lifetime, are forgotten. Less artificial than much of the old classic English verse with which he became familiar in his youth, some of its best qualities are to be remarked in his poems. Those which remain—he destroyed many—were scattered in his writings, but have been brought together in a small volume by Mr. Sanborn. He did not often reach perfect rhythmical expression, but one cannot read far in his prose without coming on the thought and words of a true poet. Walden called out these by her colour, her purity, her reflections, her ice, her children.

One morning, when she had put on her white armour against the winter, he goes down for his morning draught, axe in hand. "I cut my way first through a foot of snow, and then a foot of ice, and open a window under my feet where, kneeling to drink, I look down into the quiet parlour of the fishes, pervaded by a softened light, as through a window of ground glass with its bright sanded floor the same as in summer; there a perennial waveless serenity reigns as in the amber twilight sky, corresponding to the cool and even temperament of the inhabitants. Heaven is under our feet as well as over our heads.

"Ah, the pickerel of Walden! when I see them lying on the ice, I am always surprised by their rare beauty, as if they were fabulous fishes, they are so foreign to the streets, even to the woods, foreign as Arabia to our Concord life. They possess a quite dazzling and transcendent beauty which separates them by a wide interval from the cadaverous cod and haddock whose fame is trumpeted in our streets.[28] They are not green like the pines, nor gray like the stones, nor blue like the sky; but they have, to my eyes, if possible, yet rarer colours, like flowers and precious stones, as if they were the pearls, the animal nuclei or crystals of the Walden water. They, of course, are Walden all over and all through; are themselves small Waldens in the animal kingdom, Waldenses. It is surprising that they are caught here,—that in this deep and capacious spring, far beneath the rattling teams and chaises and tinkling sleighs that travel the Walden road, this great gold and emerald fish swims. I never chanced to see its kind in any market; it would be the cynosure of all eyes there. Easily, with a few convulsive quirks, they give up their watery ghosts, like a mortal translated before his time to the thin air of heaven."[29]

Hear the message of beauty that the telegraph-wire sung for Thoreau's ears:—

"As I went under the new telegraph wire, I heard it vibrating like a harp high overhead. It was as the sound of a far-off, glorious life, a supernal life which came down to us and vibrated the latticework of this life of ours,—an Æolian harp. . . . It seemed to me as if every pore of the wood was filled with music. As I put my ear to one of the posts, it laboured with the strains, as if every fibre was affected, and being seasoned or timed, rearranged

according to a new and more harmonious law. Every swell
and change and inflection of tone pervaded it, and seemed to
proceed from the wood, the divine tree or wood, as if its very
substance was transmuted.

"What a recipe for preserving wood, to fill its pores with music!
How this wild tree from the forest, stripped of its bark and set up
here, rejoices to transmit this music. The resounding wood,—
how much the ancients would have made of it! To have had a harp
on so great a scale, girdling the very earth, and played on by the
winds of every latitude and longitude, and that harp were (so to
speak) the manifest blessing of Heaven on a work of man's."

It seems well here to introduce some passages shedding light
on the relations of four men who, between the years 1835 and
1845, met as dwellers in our village,—though only Thoreau was
born there,—all scholars in different ways, who, afterwards,
won some fame by their lives and books.

Two newly married young men came to our quiet town to find
homes. The shy Hawthorne went to the Manse, temporarily
unoccupied by the Ripley family,[†] and the interesting though
perverse genius, William Ellery Channing, with his fair young wife
(Margaret Fuller's[††] sister), looking like a Madonna of Raphael's,
took a little house on the broad meadow just beyond Emerson's.

Thoreau with friendly courtesy did the honours of the river
and the wood to each man in turn, for he held with Emerson
that Nature says "One to one, my dear." Though Channing
remained in Concord most of his life, Hawthorne at that time
stayed but two years. Thoreau, while a homesick tutor in Staten
Island, in a letter to Emerson thus shows that friendship with
the new-comers had begun:—

[†] The family of George Ripley, a founder of the Brook Farm Community and
of *The Dial* magazine.

[††] (Sarah) Margaret Fuller (1810–50), Transcendentalist writer and critic, fem-
inist, and editor of *The Dial* (1840–42).

"Dear Friends:—I was very glad to hear your voices from so far. . . . My thoughts revert to those dear hills and that RIVER which so fills up the world to its brim,—worthy to be named with Mincius and Alpheus,—still drinking its meadows while I am far away. . . .

"I am pleased to think of Channing as an inhabitant of the gray town. Seven cities contended for Homer dead. Tell him to remain at least long enough to establish Concord's right and interest in him. . . . And Hawthorne, too, I remember as one with whom I sauntered, in old heroic times, along the banks of the Scamander, amid the ruins of chariots and heroes. Tell him not to desert, even after the tenth year. Others may say, 'Are there not the cities of Asia?' But what are they? Staying at home is the heavenly way."

In these days when the classics are misprised, the old "humanities" so crowded out by the practical, it is good to observe how this sturdy villager's life and his writing were enriched by his love of Homer, Æschylus, Simonides and Pindar.

Thoreau and Alcott always had friendly relations, though they were not drawn one to the other. Thoreau, with his hardy independence, was impatient of Alcott's philosophic calm while failing to comfortably maintain his family. This invalidated his philosophy, of which Thoreau said he "hated a sum that did not prove." These lean periods occurred when this good man could find no hearing for the spiritual mission, especially to the young, to which he felt himself called.

Thoreau helped Alcott build the really beautiful summer-house of knotted oak and twisted pine for Mr. Emerson while he was in Europe in 1847–48. He sawed deftly, and drove the nails straight for the philosopher. He was at that time living at the house as kindly protector and friend of Mrs. Emerson and the three young children, and attending to his absent friend's affairs in house, garden, and wood-lot. He wrote to Emerson: "Alcott has heard that I laughed, and set the people laughing at his arbor, though I never laughed louder than when I was on the ridge-pole. But now I have not laughed for a long time, it is so serious. He is very grave to look at. But, not knowing all this, I strove innocently enough, the other day, to engage his attention to my mathematics. 'Did you ever study geometry, the relation of straight lines to curves, the transition from the finite to the infinite? Fine things about it in Newton and Leibnitz.' But he would hear none of it,—men of taste preferred the natural curve. Ah, he is a crooked stick himself. He is getting on now so many *knots* an hour."

Emerson was a good intermediate, and valued both his friends. Four years later he wrote in his Journal:—

"I am my own man more than most men, yet the loss of a few persons would be most impoverishing, a few persons who give flesh to what were else mere thoughts, and which now I am not at liberty to slight, or in any manner treat as fictions. It were too much to say that the Platonic world I might have learned to treat as cloud-land, had I not known Alcott, who is a native of that country; yet will I say that he makes it as solid as Massachusetts to me; and Thoreau gives me, in flesh and blood and pertinacious Saxon belief, my own ethics. He is far more real, and daily practically obeying them, than I, and fortifies my memory at all times with an affirmative experience which refuses to be set aside."

To go back a little to their first acquaintance. In 1837, the boy of twenty, just graduated, and his writings, had been brought to Mrs. Emerson's notice by Mr. Emerson's sister, Mrs. Brown, who boarded with the Thoreaus. In that year, Mr. Emerson wrote: "My good Henry Thoreau made this else solitary afternoon sunny with his simplicity and clear perception. How comic is simplicity in this double-dealing, quacking world. Everything that boy says makes merry with society, though nothing can be graver than his meaning."

Here is a pleasant record of friendship in a letter written to Carlyle[†] in 1841: "One reader and friend of yours dwells now in my house, and, as I hope, for a twelvemonth to come,—Henry Thoreau,—a poet whom you may one day be proud of,—a noble, manly youth, full of melodies and inventions. We work together day by day in my garden, and I grow well and strong." The little garden which was being planted with fruit-trees and vegetables, with Mrs. Emerson's tulips and roses from Plymouth at the upper end, needed more care and much more skill to

---

†Thomas Carlyle (1795–1881), Scottish essayist and historian.

plant and cultivate than the owner had; who, moreover, could only spare a few morning hours to the work. So Thoreau took it in charge for his friend. He dealt also with the chickens, defeating their raids on the garden by asking Mrs. Emerson to make some shoes of thin morocco to stop their scratching.

This friendly alliance was a success. Emerson wrote: "Though we pine for great men, we do not use them when they come. Here is a Damascus blade of a man, such as you may search through nature in vain to parallel, laid up on a shelf in our village to rust and ruin."

Mr. Emerson was chafing at the waste of this youth in the pencil mill, and impatient for his fruiting time, surely to come. And yet he did not quite see that Thoreau was steering a course true to his compass with happy result to his voyage, a course that would for him, Emerson, have been quite unfit. Thus, in 1848, he writes: "Henry Thoreau is like the wood-god who solicits the wandering poet, and draws him into 'antres vast and desarts idle,' and leaves him naked, plaiting vines and with twigs in his hand. Very seductive are the first steps from the town to the woods, but the end is want and madness." The result was not so, and it must be remembered that Emerson recorded one mood or aspect at a time.

On a luckier day he writes: "Henry is a good substantial childe, not encumbered with himself. He has no troublesome memory, no wake, but lives extempore, and brings to-day a new proposition as radical and revolutionary as that of yesterday, but different. The only man of leisure in the town. He is a good Abbot Samson;[30] and carries counsel in his breast. If I cannot show his performance much more manifest than that of the other grand promises, at least I can see that with his practical faculty, he has declined all the kingdoms of this world. Satan has no bribe for him."

When Thoreau came, rather unwillingly, by invitation to dine with company, it often happened that he was in a captious mood, amusing himself by throwing paradoxes in the way of the smooth current of the conversation. It was like having Pan at a dinner party.[31] Even when he "dropped in" to the study at the end of the afternoon, and had told the last news from the river or Fairhaven Hill, Mr. Emerson, at a later period, complained that Thoreau baulked his effort "to hold intercourse with his mind." With all their honour for one another, and their Spartan affection, satisfactory talks then seem to have been rare. But a long afternoon's ramble with Pan guiding to each sight, or sound, or fragrance, perhaps to be found only on that day, was dear privilege, and celebrated as such by Emerson in his journals.

But even Pan "took sides" when Liberty was in peril, the Greek tradition tells us,[32] and so did his Concord followers. In the dark days of 1853 Mr. Emerson wrote: "I go for those who have received a retaining fee to this party of Freedom before they came into the world. I would trust Garrison,[†] I would trust Henry Thoreau, that they would make no compromises."

It is good to know that it has been recorded of Alcott, the benign idealist, that when the Reverend Thomas Wentworth Higginson (later, a Colonel in the Northern Army), heading the rush on the United States Court House in Boston to rescue the fugitive slave, looked back for his following at the Court-room door, only the apostolic philosopher was there, cane in hand.

But Thoreau had qualities which the Platonist lacked. Emerson, writing of Mother-wit, says,—"Doctor Johnson, Milton, Chaucer and Burns had it. Aunt Mary Moody Emerson has it, and can write scrap letters. Who has it need never write anything but scraps. Henry Thoreau has it."

When "Walden" appeared Mr. Emerson seems to have felt as much pleasure as if his brother had written it. But when the Thoreau family, after Henry's death, submitted the journals to his friend's consideration, he, coming from his study, day by day, would tell his children his joyful surprise in the merit and the beauty which he found everywhere in those daily chronicles of Nature and of thought.

The virtue of Thoreau has always commanded respect; of his knowledge of Natural History, Lowell alone, as far as I know, has spoken slightingly. But his views of life,—when these are referred to, how often it is with a superior smile. True the fault

---

†William Lloyd Garrison (1805–79), Abolitionist leader who published a news-paper, *The Liberator*, 1831–65.

lies partly with Thoreau, that his Scotch pugnacity sometimes betrayed him into rhetorical over-statement and he would not stoop to qualify: thought a maximum dose of bitter-tonic, in the condition of society in his day, would do it no harm. But let us also bethink ourselves before we give final judgment. Might not modesty whisper that some of us, the critics, live on a lower plane, and that the *point of view* made a difference? May not a man on a hill see that his friends below, though apparently on a clear ascending path, will soon come to thickets and ravines, while by taking what looks like a wildcat path to them they will soon reach the height? Have the conduct and words of most poets, prophets, even of the founders of the great religions, been considered sagacious "on 'Change"?

When one sees another, helpful and kindly in common relations, sincere and brave in speech, and ever trying to keep the conversation above gossip and triviality; easily earning a simple living by work, humble, but done as if for God's inspection, yet saving a share of each day for the life to which his instinct and genius lead him, yet, on occasion, leaving it readily to please and help others; able to rise above bitter bereavement; using disappointment in early love to purify life; fearless and in good heart in life and in death,—one may well ask, Is Folly behind all this?

Make allowance for strong statement due to any original, vigorous man, trying to arouse his neighbours from lethargy to freedom and happiness that he believed within their reach, and then, with the perspective of years to help us, look fairly at the main lines of his life and thought, which have been considered so strange and *outré*.

Consider the standards of education and religion in New England in Thoreau's youth,—the position of the churches, their distrust of the right of the individual to question the words of the Bible as interpreted by the Sects; the horror that Theodore Parker[†] inspired, the shyness of the so-called Pagan

---

[†]A Unitarian theologian, pastor, and social reformer (1810–60), he was an active Abolitionist.

Scriptures, the difficulty with which any one who spoke for
the slave could get a hearing, the ridicule of the so-called
Transcendentalists, the general practice of what is now called,
"pauperizing Mediæval Charity," the indignant rejection of
Evolution theories, the slight taste for Natural History, and the
astonishment that a rich family "camping out" would have excited.
Now we have long had intelligent system in schools, and voca-
tional instruction too, and electives in the Universities; we blush
to remember the rendition of Sims and Burns, John Brown has
been almost canonized by some people as the John Baptist of
Freedom's Triumph; the *Dial* is spoken of with respect, the
memory of Theodore Parker is honoured in the churches, the
"Light of Asia" read as a religious work, Mediæval alms-giving,
we are told by the Associated Charities, is a sin; the so-called
"lower animals" have their companions, yea, are practically
owned as ancestors; and when a party is found under the greenwood tree no Orlando would say, now,—

> "Whate'er you are
> That in this desert inaccessible
> Under the shade of melancholy boughs
> Lose and neglect the creeping hours of Time;
> If ever you have looked on better days,
> If ever been where bells have knolled to
>   church," etc.

but, on the contrary, knows that they are trying to preserve or
regain their sanity after a season of lecture, party, street-car,
and telephone life. "Who laughs last, laughs best." Was society
wrong in his day, or Thoreau?

This rare and happy venture of Thoreau's,—bringing his soul
face to face with Nature as wondrous artist, as healer, teacher, as
mediator between us and the Creator, has slowly spread its wide
beneficence. Look at out-of-door life, and love of plant and tree,
and sympathy with animals, now, as compared with these seventy
years ago. Yet to-day the inestimable value of frequent solitude
is much overlooked.

He devoutly listened. He writes in his Journal: "If I do not
keep step with others, it is because I hear a different drummer.

Let a man step to the music which he hears, however measured, and however far away."

Again: "If within the old man there is not a young man,—within the sophisticated one, an unsophisticated one,—then he is but one of the Devil's angels."

When we read the poems that have become great classics describing the man, pure, constant and upright; David's "Lord, who shall abide in Thy tabernacle?" the "Integer Vitæ" of Horace, Sir Henry Wotton's—

> "How happy is he born and taught,
> Who serveth not another's will";—

or Herbert's "Constancie,"—to one who knew Henry Thoreau well, whose image would more quickly arise than his? Does one need to labor to prove that he had a religion?

Read his acknowledgment of the sudden coming of spiritual help,—

> "It comes in Summer's broadest noon,
> By a grey wall, in some chance place,
> Unseasoning in time, insulting June,
> And vexing day with its presuming face.
>
> "I hearing get, who had but ears,
> And sight, who had but eyes before;
> I moments live, who lived but years,
> And truth discern, who knew but learning's lore.
>
> "I will not doubt the love untold,
> Which not my worth or want hath bought,
> Which woed me young, and woes me old,
> And to this evening hath me brought."

Thoreau was but forty-four years old when he died. Even his health could not throw off a chill got by long stooping in a wet snow storm counting the growth-rings on the stumps of some old trees. The family infection became active. He lived a year and a half after this exposure and made a trip to Minnesota in vain for health. For the last months he was confined to the house, he was affectionate, and utterly brave, and worked on his manuscript until the last days. When his neighbour, Reverend Mr. Reynolds, came in he found him so employed, and he looked up cheerfully and, with a twinkle in his eye, whispered— his voice was gone—"you know it's respectable to leave an estate to one's friends.[33] His old acquaintance Staples, once his jailor, coming out, meeting Mr. Emerson coming in, reported that he "never saw a man dying with so much pleasure and peace." To his Calvinistic Aunt who felt obliged to ask, "Henry, have you made your peace with God?"—"I did not know we had ever quarrelled, Aunt," was the pleasant answer.

His friend and companion, Edward Hoar, said to me, "With Thoreau's life something went out of Concord woods and fields and river that never will return. He so loved Nature, delighted in her every aspect and seemed to infuse himself into her." Yes, something went. But our woods and waters will always be different because of this man. Something of him abides and truly "for good" in his town. Here he was born, and within its borders he found a wealth of beauty and interest—all that he asked—and shared it with us all.[34]

In his day, as now too, was much twilight, and men were slaves to their fears and to hobgoblins. Taking for his motto,—

"Make courage for life to be Capitaine Chief,"

he, with truth and Nature to help him, cut a way through to freedom.

"He looked up to a mountain tract
And saw that every morning, far withdrawn
Beyond the darkness and the cataract,
God made himself an awful rose of Dawn,
Unheeded; yes, for many a month and year
Unheeded ever."

But not by him. He learned this, he says, by his experiment of a life with Nature simply followed for his guide; that "if one advances confidently in the direction of his dreams, and endeavours to live the life that he has imagined, he will meet with a success unexpected in common hours. He will put some things behind, will pass an invisible boundary; new, universal, and more liberal laws will begin to establish themselves around and within him; or the old laws will be expanded and interpreted in his favour in a more liberal sense, and he will live with the license of a higher order of beings. In proportion as he simplifies his life, the laws of the universe will appear less complex, and solitude will not be solitude, nor poverty poverty, nor weakness weakness. If you have built castles in the air, your work need not be lost; that is where they should be. Now put the foundations under them."

This man, in his lifetime little known, except outwardly, even in his own town, whose books were returned to him as unsalable, is better known and prized more nearly at his worth each year, and to-day is giving freedom and joy in life to fellowmen in the far parts of this country, and beyond the ocean. Let us not misprize him, and regret that he did not make pencils and money. Something of his strange early prayer was granted. It was this:—

> "Great God, I ask thee for no meaner pelf
> Than that I may not disappoint myself;
> That in my action I may soar as high
> As I can now discern with this clear eye.
> And, next in value which thy kindness lends,
> That I may—greatly—disappoint my friends,
> Howe'er they think or hope that it may be,
> They may not dream how thou'st distinguished me.
> That my weak hand may equal my firm faith,
> And my life practise more than my tongue saith;
> That my low conduct may not show,
> Nor my relenting lines,
> That I thy purpose did not know
> Or overrated thy designs."[35]

Notes

1. Thoreau writes in his journal: "We linger in manhood to tell the dreams of our childhood, and they are half forgotten ere we acquire the faculty of expressing them."

2. Lowell never had any but the slightest acquaintance with Thoreau. During his rustication in Concord he had probably been prejudiced by village criticism of Thoreau's independent ways. Lowell also was distinctly a "society man" and would have been unsympathetic with this rustic oddity. In the *Fable for Critics* he ridicules Thoreau as an imitator. Years later, in his essay, he treats with a superior levity, through more than half of his pages, this brave and serious man. In two or three pages at the end he gives praise which should make all the previous criticism dust in the balance. Unhappy the neutral public will be prepossessed by the wit and have formed their opinions on the first portion. But Lowell's Essay, like Stevenson's, written on imperfect knowledge, remains, and has influenced many people. There is good reason to think that his opinion in later years changed.

But Lowell must be credited with this high praise of Thoreau's quality as a writer:—"With every exception there is no writing comparable with Thoreau's in kind, that is comparable with it in degree where it is best. His range was narrow, but to be a master is to be a master. There are sentences of his as perfect as anything in the language, and thoughts as clearly crystallized; his metaphors and images are always fresh from the soil."

3. The late Mr. Horace Hosmer, of Acton, a very interesting man, whose valuable reminiscences of the Thoreau brothers as teachers of the Academy will be given later, kindly sent me, in 1890, the following:—

> *Notes and jottings, impressions of Thoreau*
> *Family, etc.,—for Edward W. Emerson*
> *by Horace R. Hosmer*

"That H. D. Thoreau was not a superior scion on an inferior stock; neither was he begotten by a northwest wind as many have supposed.

"That there were good and sufficient reasons for the children's taste for Botany and Natural History. 'The aspirations of parents often become realizations in the children'; John Thoreau and wife were seen year after year on the west bank of the Assabet, on Fairhaven, Lee's Hill, [Nashawtuc] and at Walden. My mother said that one of the children narrowly escaped being born on Lee's Hill. I never knew or heard of Mrs. Thoreau taking a *second grade* of anything willingly.

"That John Thoreau satisfied *her,* and that he begat as much brains as was fashionable in those days; that his hand writing was beautiful, that his pencils, marbled paper, stove polish, plumbago for electro-typing was the best in the market.

"That his negative nature coupled with the positive of his wife pro-duced good results. Was remarkably cautious and secretive.

"That the light which he hid under a bushel was worth more than the personal and real estate of Concord *at that time.* John, Jr., was his father turned inside out.

"Am satisfied that I misconstrued Henry's silence concerning John. [The young Hosmer, at the time, felt that Thoreau did not care as much as he, who almost worshipped John.] I honestly believed that John was the Architect and Henry only wrought out his plans, and think so yet. Jesus had Paul."

4. Thoreau took the Bachelor of Arts, but never the Master of Arts degree, and very properly. For in his day, and for at least thirty years after, the possession of the latter parchment only signified that one's vitality had held out to burn for three years, and that one could spare five dollars to the University.

5. This scholar was Horace R. Hosmer, whose account of the senior Thoreaus has been already quoted. His older brother had also been a pupil. Hosmer wrote to me as follows:—

"Every one in that school had their duties assigned, as on a Cunard steamer, and did their own part.

"When I first came, a little boy, John said 'I want you to be a good boy and study, because you are my friend's little brother.' Soon after, I was called to his desk by John. He had spoken to me once or twice, but I had not heard, and he thought I was sulky. I said I had not heard him, and he looked at me and believed me, and to make amends opened his desk and took out *Lazy Lawrence* and gave it to me to read.

"When the second term was to begin, he said to me, 'If your father doesn't feel able to send you next term, you come, and you shall have your tuition free.'

"Sometimes he used to take me by the hand and lead me home to dinner. I never forgot those dinners; the room was shaded and cool, there was no hustle. Mrs. Thoreau's bread, brown and white, was the best I had ever tasted. They had, beside, vegetables and fruit, pies or puddings; but I never saw meat there. [The Thoreaus were not vegetarians exclusively, but this was at a time of saving.] Their living was a revelation to me. I think they were twenty years ahead of the times in Concord.

"At the house there was nothing jarring. Mrs. Thoreau was pleasant and talkative and her husband was always kind. If I ever saw a gentle-man at home, it was he. John would carry melons from his garden for the scholars. Once I found a piece of melon in my desk and should have supposed it was put there as a joke, but I caught the fragrance. It was the first citron melon I ever had seen.

"In reading about Arnold of Rugby I have often thought that John Thoreau resembled him in conducting his school. To me that man seemed to make all things possible. Henry was not loved in the school. He had his scholars upstairs. I was with John only. John was the more human, loving; understood and thought of others. Henry thought more about himself. He was a conscientious teacher but rigid." . . . Here follows the passage, quoted in the text, of Henry's then being "in the green-apple stage."

As I parted from Mr. Hosmer, whom the memory of his loved master had deeply stirred, he exclaimed, "When I hear of Henry Thoreau's growing fame the lines in Byron's 'Isles of Greece' from our old Reading Book rise in my mind,—

> 'Ye have the Pyrrhic dance as yet,—
> Where is the Pyrrhic phalanx gone?
> Of two such lessons why forget
> The nobler and the manlier one?'"

And the tears stood in his eyes.

6. This pupil was Dr. Thomas Hosmer of Bedford, for many years a practitioner of dentistry in Boston. He and another Bedford boy, B. W. Lee, later of Newport, Vermont, used to walk to the Academy, four miles, and back, every day and were praised for never having been absent or tardy. In winter they could skate up the river part way. Henry taught the older classes Latin and Greek, also Natural Philosophy. Both of these boys valued the school and their teachers highly.

Mr. Lee wrote to me, "There is one thing which I shall never forget of them, and that is their kindness and good will shown me while at their school, and their great desire to impress upon the minds of their scholars to do right always."

Dr. Hosmer added this pleasant picture to his story of Henry: "I have seen children catch him by the hand, as he was going home from school, to walk with him and hear more."

Thoreau's morning talks, Dr. Hosmer said, "showed that he knew himself there to teach broadly, and to awaken thought,—not merely to hear lessons in the rudiments of letters."

7. Henry thus treated of profanity: "Boys, if you went to talk business with a man, and he persisted in thrusting words having no connection with the subject into all parts of every sentence—Boot-jack, for instance,—wouldn't you think he was taking a liberty with you, and trifling with your time, and wasting his own?" He then introduced the "Boot-jack" violently and frequently into a sentence, to illustrate the absurdity of street bad language in a striking way.

8. Mr. George Keyes, of Concord, spoke of that school as "very pleasant indeed." He told me that the brothers organized a survey of

Fairhaven Hill in Concord and the river-shore below it, to give the boys an idea of the field-work of surveying, and the use of instruments. In this he remembers Henry as the more active of the two.

Mr. Keyes said: "We boys used to visit him on Saturday afternoons at his house by Walden, and he would show us interesting things in the woods near by. I did not see the philosophical side. He was never stern or pedantic, but natural and very agreeable, friendly,—but a person you would never feel inclined to fool with. A face that you would long remember. Though short in stature, and inconspicuous in dress, you would not fail to notice him in the street, as more than ordinary."

9. Thoreau sent to his friend a copy of these verses. In Mr. Emerson's journal for August, 1839, is written: "Last night came to me a beautiful poem from Henry Thoreau, 'Sympathy.' The purest strain, and the loftiest, I think, that has yet pealed from this unpoetic American forest. I hear his verses with as much triumph as I point to my Guido when they praise half poets and half painters." [Carlyle had sent to Mr. and Mrs. Emerson a fine engraving of The Aurora.]

Three years later, the older friend was more exacting in his praise of the younger. In November, 1842, he wrote: "Henry Thoreau wrote me verses which pleased, if not by beauty of particular lines, yet by the honest truth, and by the length of flight and strength of wing, for most of our poets are only writers of lines or of epigrams. These of Henry's at least have rude strength, and we do not come to the bottom of the mine. Their fault is that the gold does not yet flow pure, but is drossy and crude. The thyme and marjoram are not yet made into honey."

10. Thoreau wrote soon after little Waldo's death to Mrs. Emerson's sister:—

"As for Waldo, he died as the mist rises from the brook which the sun will soon dart his rays through. Do not the flowers die every autumn? He had not even taken root here. I was not startled to hear that he was dead; it seemed the most natural thing that could happen. His fine organization demanded it, and Nature gently yielded his request. It would have been strange if he had lived."

11. In 1843, after he had lived more than a year with the Emersons, Thoreau went to Staten Island as tutor to one of Mr. William Emerson's sons for several months. After his return, Mr. Emerson went to England and again he kindly came to live and look after things in his friend's home. After Mr. Emerson's return his daughter Ellen, ten years old, the eldest child, went to visit her Staten Island relatives. Thoreau, perhaps remembering his homesickness while there, kindly wrote the following home letter to the little girl:—

Concord, July 31, 1849.

Dear Ellen,—

I think that we are pretty well acquainted, though we never had any very long talks. We have had a good many short talks, at any rate. Don't you remember how we used to despatch our breakfasts two winters ago, as soon as Eddy could get on his feeding-tire, which was not always remembered before the rest of the household had come down? Don't you remember our wise criticisms on the pictures in the portfolio and the Turkish book, with Eddy and Edith looking on,—how almost any pictures answered our purpose and we went through the *Penny Magazine*, first from beginning to end, and then from end to beginning, and Eddy stared just as much the second time as the first, and Edith thought that we turned over too soon, and that there were some things which she had not seen? I can guess pretty well what interests you and what you think about. Indeed I am interested in pretty much the same things myself. I suppose you think that persons who are as old as your father and myself are always thinking about very grave things, but I know that we are meditating the same old themes that we did when we were ten years old, only we go more gravely about it. You love to write or to read a fairy story, and that is what you will always like to do, in some form or other. By and by you will discover that you want what are called the necessaries of life only that you may realize some such dream.

Eddy has got him a fish-pole and line with a pin-hook at the end, which he flourishes over the dry ground and the carpet at the risk of tearing out our eyes; but when I told him that he must have a cork and a sinker, his mother took off the pin and tied on a cork instead; but he doubts whether that will catch fish as well. He tells me that he is five years old. Indeed I was present at the celebration of his birth-day lately, and supplied the company with onion and squash pipes, and rhubarb whistles, which is the most I can do on such occasions. Little Sammy Hoar blowed them most successfully, and made the loudest noise, though it almost strained his eyes out to do it. Edith is full of spirits. When she comes home from school she goes hop, skip and jump down into the field to pick berries, currants, gooseberries, raspberries, and thimbleberries; if there is one of these that has thoughts of changing its hue by to-morrow morning, I guess that Edith knows something about it and will consign it to her basket for Grandmama.

Children may now be seen going a-berrying in all directions. The white-lilies are in blossom, and the john'swort and goldenrod are beginning to come out. Old people say that we have not had so warm a summer for thirty years. Several persons have died in consequence of the heat,—Mr. Kendal, perhaps for one. The Irishmen on the railroad were obliged to leave off their work for several days, and the farmers left their fields and sought the shade. William Brown of the poor house is dead,—the one who used to ask for a cent—"Give me a cent?" I wonder who will have his cents now!

I found a nice penknife on the bank of the river this afternoon, which was probably lost by some villager who went there to bathe lately. Yesterday I found a nice arrowhead, which was lost some time before by an Indian who was hunting there. The knife was a very little rusted; the arrowhead was not rusted at all.

You must see the sun rise out of the ocean before you come home. I think that Long Island will not be in the way, if you climb to the top of the hill—at least, no more than Bolster Island, and Pillow Hills, and even the Lowlands of Never-get-up are elsewhere.

Do not think that you must write to me because I have written to you. It does not follow at all. You would not naturally make so long a speech to me here in a month as a letter would be. Yet if some time it should be perfectly easy and pleasant to you, I shall be very glad to have a sentence.

Your old acquaintance,
Henry Thoreau.

12. This passage in Mr. Emerson's journal in 1834 carries us back to the young mechanic period: "Henry Thoreau said he knew but one secret, which was, to do one thing at a time, and, though he has his evenings for study, if he was in the day inventing machines for sawing his plumbago, he invents wheels all the evening and night also; and if this week he has some good reading and thoughts before him his brain runs on that all day whilst pencils pass through his hands."

13. In 1890, I talked with Mr. Warren Miles of Concord, who, having worked with the Munroes, earlier pencil-makers of Concord, came into the employ of John Thoreau, Sr. He told me that the graphite came from the Tudor Mine at Sturbridge for many years, until that mine was closed. Later, it was procured from Canada, but was not so good. It seems that the Germans got their lead, such as is used in the Fabers' pencil, from Ceylon. Miles suggested the improvement of stones, instead of iron balls, for grinding. Presumably this was after the Thoreaus' invention of the air-blast which gave the wonderfully fine powder to which they owed their success, for, before that, the grit of the stones would have spoiled the product. Mr. Miles thinks that John Thoreau, Sr., may have thought of the air-blast plan, but that Henry at any rate worked out the details. Mr. Miles took me to his mill to see the perfection and simplicity of the operation.

Mr. Horace Hosmer, who, for a time, was the travelling selling agent of the pencils, stated that the Bavarian clay was used here at that time by the New England Glass Company, and by the Phœnix Crucible Company of Taunton. Perhaps the Thoreaus bought it through these companies. The old pencils were filled by applying the warm mixture of graphite, glue and spermaceti or bayberry wax with a brush to the grooved half of the pencil. The Thoreaus' clay and graphite mixture, after casting into "leads," hardened like stone and could stand intense heat.

14. Thoreau writes: "Explore your own higher latitudes; nay, be a Columbus to whole new continents and worlds within you, opening new channels, not of trade, but of thought. Every man is lord of a realm beside which the earthly empire of the Czar is but a petty state.

I do not wish to be any more busy with my hands than is necessary. My head is hands and feet. I feel all my best faculties concentrated in it. My instinct tells me that my head is an organ for burrowing, as some creatures used their snout and fore-paws, and with it I would mine and burrow my way through these hills. I think that *the richest vein is somewhere hereabouts:* so by the divining rod and thin rising vapours I judge: and here I will begin to mine."

Again: "If my curve is large, why bend it to a smaller circle?"

Emerson wrote of Thoreau: "He who sees the horizon may securely say what he pleases of any twig or tree between him and it."

15. "The Regicides," Edward Goffe and William Whalley, distinguished officers under Cromwell, who, proscribed after the Restoration, fled to New England and with a price set on their heads lived to old age hidden among the hills near Hadley and New Haven.

16. Allusion has been made to the time when Staples became Emerson's next neighbour and on the survey it appeared that the partition ditch was well over on the land of the latter. The matter being generously settled, Thoreau came into the house and sat down to rest in the study. He said: "I like Sam Staples; he has no hypocrisy about him. He has just been telling me how he came to Concord, nineteen years old, after a hard-worked boyhood, looking for a job. He had just a ninepence [they were then in use], and he went over to the tavern and spent half of it for rum, and he says it started him right, and in good spirits." The youth's steady advance from then to the day of his death ought not to make a good Sunday-School book, First, he was hostler, soon promoted to bar-keeper and clerk, then married the only daughter of the innkeeper; was chosen constable. Concord was then a shire-town and as judges, lawyers, jurymen, and witnesses had all made pleasant acquaintance with him in his honest dispensing of spirituous comforts, he was appointed jailor, and was a most able, humane and intelligent one, also tax-collector. Mr. Emerson had performed his marriage ceremony, and, as Alcott and John S. Dwight happened to be with him, they were present as witnesses in the "old Middlesex" parlor. Staples, later, confounded Dwight with the Englishman Wright (of the Fruitlands colony), so, in his old age, telling me the story, added, "I had both of 'em in my jail soon after." His steady friendship for Thoreau, his first prisoner for conscience' sake, and his distinctly unsympathetic relation with Dr. Alcott whom, with entire kindness, he spoke of as "a regular dude," have been told.

A few years later he was chosen Representative in the General Court, and twice reëlected, serving sensibly and well on the Committees on Prisons and on Accounts. When the Court and jail were moved to Lowell, Staples became an auctioneer, real estate man, and farmer, but will be remembered perhaps chiefly as a kindly neighbour, advisor of unpractical people of all degrees in our village family, especially of widows and lone women. He called almost every one by their first names and it was not taken amiss. He was a genial member of the Social Circle. Once at one of their evening gatherings, the late Judge Keyes spoke of the interesting composition of the Club,—two ministers, three judges, one lawyer, one doctor, and so on through the list, ending "and one gentleman." Immediately the chorus "Who's that, Judge?" rose, for we all were sure we were otherwise accounted for. "Why, Sam there. He's our one retired gentleman," said the judge. When, a few years later, in the winter of 1894–95, we lost Judge Hoar, Rev. Mr. Reynolds, and Mr. Staples, we felt as if a tripod upholding Concord's high standards and kindly, simple life had fallen.

17. The late George Bradford Bartlett remembered Thoreau's coming often to his father, good Doctor Bartlett's house. He did so the night after his release from prison. George felt as if he were seeing a Siberian exile, or John Bunyan.

He said that Henry often did carpentry jobs, etc., for his father. The Doctor furnished a fence for poor Mrs. O'Brien, opposite the New Burying-ground, and Thoreau made it, with George's boyish help. He used to visit Thoreau at Walden and remembers how the house was arranged. He recalls his pausing to hear songs of distant birds, telling what bird it was, and whether male or female, that sung or chirped; also calling attention to insect sounds, and his inferring the insect's state of mind. He recalled the sudden increase of Thoreau's library by his receiving upwards of four hundred volumes of the *Week* back from the publishers, and Mr. Emerson's saying, "The day will come when this will be famous as Gilbert White's *Notes of Selborne*," was more than fulfilled. Mr. Bartlett also told me that, in Pennsylvania, he had met a student, a Russian Jew, who was eager to see him, as a man who had known Thoreau. This man said that, in his early youth, in Russia, he had read one of Thoreau's books, and it had determined him to become a free man and helped him through the toil and danger required. His desire was to translate Thoreau's works into Russian.

18. Thoreau had earlier objected to a man's deliberately putting himself into an attitude of opposition to the laws of society, or of the land, but rather felt it his duty to "maintain himself, in whatever attitude he find himself through obedience to the laws of his being, which will never be one of opposition to a just government, if he should chance to meet with such." Now, every sense of the man rebelled at the official attitude of his country with regard to human slavery.

19. But the judge, as in duty bound, explained to the Jury that this law had been regularly enacted by Congress, approved by the President, and held to be valid by the Supreme Court; hence, that all citizens were in practice legally bound to obey it. He admitted that

even a Republic might pass a wicked law. "If a statute is passed which any citizen, examining his duty by the best light which God has given him, . . . believes to be wicked, and which, acting under the law of God, he thinks he ought to disobey, unquestionably he ought to disobey that statute, because he ought to 'obey God rather than man.' . . . But, gentlemen, a man whose private conscience leads him to disobey a law recognized by the community must take the consequences of that disobedience. It is a matter solely between him and his Maker. . . . It will not do for the public authorities to recognize his private opinion as a justification of his acts."

Emerson said, in public, at this period: "The Union is at an end so soon as an immoral law is enacted, and he who writes a crime into the statute-book digs under the foundations of the Capitol, to plant there a powder magazine, and lays a train."

20. Mr. Henry S. Salt, who, in 1890, published in London his excellent and appreciative book on Thoreau, tells how in the same essay Stevenson summed up his character by the phrase "a skulker" but had to admit later—unhappily only in a preface—that he had quite misread Thoreau through lack of sufficient knowledge of his life.

21. Thoreau once said: "A thought would destroy, like the jet of a blow-pipe, most persons."

22. A lady who, from her youth upward, was constantly meeting Thoreau at the homes of two of his friends where she also often stayed, and who also was in friendly relation with his mother and sister, says: "When others say of Henry Thoreau that he took no interest except in his selfish concerns, that he was a mere hermit, that he was strange, indolent, had no occupation, immediately it comes to me that that is all wrong. It seems as if he had so much affection, was cordial with his kind, that is, when they were of his kind, where there were points of interest.

"He took great pleasure in learning from Nature and he wished to divide what he learned with others, and to help let them see with his eyes, that is, show them how to see."

Thoreau wrote in his journal: "It is always a recommendation to me to know that a man has ever been poor, has been regularly born into this world; knows the language. . . . I require to be assured of certain philosophers that they have once been bare-footed, have eaten a crust because they had nothing better."

23. Thoreau, living by Walden, wrote: "In a pleasant spring morning all men's sins are forgiven. Such a day is a truce to vice. While such a sun holds out to burn, the vilest sinner may return. Through our own recovered innocence we discern the innocence of our neighbours. You may have known your neighbour yesterday for a thief, a drunkard, or a sensualist, and merely pitied or despised him, and despaired of the world; but the sun shines bright and warm this spring morning, recreating the

world, and you meet him at some serene work, and see how his
exhausted and debauched veins expand with still joy and bless the new
day, feel the spring influence with the innocence of infancy, and all his
faults are forgotten. There is not only an atmosphere of good-will
about him, but even a savour of holiness groping for expression,
blindly and ineffectually perhaps, like a new-born instinct, and for a
short hour the south hill-side echoes to no vulgar jest. You see some
innocent fair shoots preparing to burst from his gnarled rind and try
another year's life, tender and fresh as the youngest plant. Even he has
entered into the joy of his lord. Why the jailor does not leave open his
prison doors,—why the judge does not dismiss his case,—why the
preacher does not dismiss his congregation. It is because they do not
obey the hint that God gives them, nor accept the pardon that he
freely offers to all."

24. The "River Fisherman" was written by Mrs. Edith Emerson
Forbes.

25. Thoreau wrote in his journal: "There are poets of all kinds and
degrees, little known to each other. The Lake School is not the only, or
the principal one. They love various things; some love beauty, and some
love rum. Some go to Rome,—and some go a-fishing, and are sent to
the house of correction once a month. They keep up their fires by
means unknown to me. I know not their comings and goings. I know
them wild, and ready to risk all when their muse invites. I meet these
gods of the river and woods with sparkling faces (like Apollo's), late
from the house of correction, it may be,—carrying whatever mystic
and forbidden bottles or other vessels concealed; while the dull, regular priests are steering their parish rafts in a prose mood. What care I
to see galleries full of representations of heathen gods, when I can see
actual living ones by an infinitely superior artist?"
He loved the River: "It is my own highway, the only wild and
unfenced part of the world hereabouts." But always he looked for
something behind what he saw. At another time he writes: "Time is but
the stream I go a-fishing in. I drink at it, but while I drink I see the
sandy bottom and detect how shallow it is. Its thin current glides away,
but eternity remains. I would drink deeper; fish in the sky whose bottom is pebbly with stars."

26. In the year of Our Lord, 1852, the alleged manifestations of
departed spirits reached Concord, through various humble "medi-
ums." Judge Hoar remarked, "If this be a treasure, verily we have it in
earthen vessels."
Thoreau writes to his sister, in Bangor: "Concord is just as idiotic as
ever in relation to the spirits and their knockings. Most people here
believe in a spiritual world which no respectable junk bottle, which

had not met with a slip, would condescend to contain even a portion of for a moment,—whose atmosphere would extinguish a candle let down into it, like a well that wants airing; in spirits which the very bull-frogs in our meadows would blackball. Their evil genius is seeing how low it can degrade them. The hooting of owls, the croaking of frogs, is celestial wisdom in comparison. If I could be brought to believe in the things which they believe, I should make haste to get rid of my certificate of stock in this and the next world's enterprises, and buy a share in the first Immediate Annihilation Company that offered. I would exchange my immortality for a glass of small beer this hot weather. Where *are* the heathen? Was there ever any superstition before? And yet I suppose there may be a vessel this very moment setting sail from the coast of Africa with a missionary on board! Consider the dawn and the sunrise,—the rainbow and the evening,—the words of Christ and the aspiration of all the saints! Hear music! see, smell, taste, feel, hear,—anything,—and then hear these idiots, inspired by the cracking of a restless board, humbly asking. 'Please, Spirit, if you cannot answer by knocks, answer by tips of the table.'!!!!!!!"

27. Through his neighbour Channing, Thoreau formed a friendship with the Ricketson family living near New Bedford, kindly people of high ideals, simple life, and lovers of Nature. The region about their home by the blue waters of Buzzard's Bay and in its softer air made a pleasant change in spring or autumn, and Thoreau found himself much at home there. He was interested not only in the parents, but their boys, one of whom made, long after Thoreau's death, the admirable bust of him of which I am permitted to use the photograph. He helped them in the alterations of their fishing boat and sailed with them. While Thoreau was visiting this family Mrs. Ricketson, playing on the piano, asked him if he cared for music and whether he sang. "Yes," he answered, "I am fond of music, and when I am in the woods I sometimes sing." She asked him to sing to the family. He answered, "Oh, I fear if I do I shall take the roof of the house off." His hostess urged him, and sat down to play the accompaniment, and he sang his favorite "Tom Bowling" with spirit and feeling, giving the full sentiment of the verses.

Alcott and George William Curtis were both visiting Mr. Ricketson, and interesting discourse had gone on at the dinner, Thoreau talking very well. After dinner, Alcott and Curtis went with Mr. Ricketson to his "Shanty" for serious talk, but the others went into the parlor to consult some bird book. Mrs. Ricketson, playing at her piano, struck into "The Campbells are Coming." Thoreau put down his book and began to dance—a sylvan dance, as of a faun among rocks and bushes in a sort of labyrinthine fashion, now leaping over obstacles, then advancing with stately strides, returning in curves, then coming back in leaps. Alcott, coming in, stood thunderstruck to see "Thoreau acting his feelings in motion" as he called it. Alcott did not have that kind of feelings.

28. The fishman, in those days, proclaimed his advent by blasts on a long tin horn, as he drove his covered wagon through the country roads. Only towns near the seashore had fishmarkets.

29. The pickerel of Walden, now nearly, if not quite, extinct, who lived in that pure water supplied by springs at the bottom, were quite different from those of the sluggish and more weedy river, with its darker water. The latter seemed of less delicate lines, and were of a dark, more muddy green, while the Walden pickerel were more silvery, and the green, as I recall it, was very pure, light and iridescent.

30. Abbot Samson is the hero in Carlyle's Past and Present.

31. On my birthday, in the early summer, just before I went to take my examination for Harvard, my father and mother invited Thoreau and Channing, both, but especially Thoreau, friends from my babyhood, to dine with us. When we left the table and were passing into the parlour, Thoreau asked me to come with him to our East door—our more homelike door, facing the orchard. It was an act of affectionate courtesy, for he had divined my suppressed state of mind and remembered that first crisis in his own life, and the wrench that it seemed in advance, as a gate leading out into an untried world. With serious face, but with a very quiet, friendly tone of voice, he reassured me, told me that I should be really close to home; very likely should pass my life in Concord. It was a great relief.

32. The legend is beautifully given by Browning in his "Pheidippides."

33. Mr. Reynolds also told how, speaking of Indian arrow-heads, he asked Thoreau if they were not rather hard to find. He said, "Yes, rather hard, but at six cents apiece I could make a comfortable living out of them."

Mr. Reynolds added: "Thoreau was one of the pleasantest gentlemen, most social and agreeable, I ever met. When I officiated at his father's funeral he came over the next evening as a courteous acknowledgment, and spent two hours, and told his Canada story far better than in his book."

From his window Thoreau could see the quiet river. Mr. Emerson, coming home from a visit to him during the last weeks of his life, wrote,—

"Henry praised to me the manners of an old, established, calm, well-behaved river, as distinguished from those of a new river. A new river is a torrent, an old one slow and steadily supplied. What happens in any part of an old river relates to what befalls in every other part of it. 'T is full of compensations, resources and reserved funds."

34. The news of Thoreau's death came to Louisa Alcott, then nursing in a military hospital. In the watches of the night, sitting by the cot of a dying soldier, her thoughts wandered back to the happy evenings when Thoreau might bring his flute with him to please the growing girls, when he visited the elders; that yellow flute, very melodious in its tone, which his brother John used to play. In these sad surroundings she wrote:—

Thoreau's Flute

We sighing said, "Our Pan is dead—
His pipe hangs mute beside the river,
Around it friendly moonbeams quiver,
But music's airy voice is fled.
Spring comes to us in guise forlorn,
The blue-bird chants a requiem,
The willow-blossom waits for him,
The genius of the wood is gone"

Then from the flute, untouched by hands,
There came a low, harmonious breath:
For such as he there is no death.
His life the eternal life commands.
Above men's aims his nature rose.
The wisdom of a just content
Made one small spot a continent,
And turned to poetry life's prose

Haunting the hills, the stream, the wild,
Swallow and aster, lake and pine
To him seemed human or divine,
Fit mates for this large-hearted child.
Such homage Nature ne'er forgets;
And yearly on the coverlid
'Neath which her darling lieth hid
Will write his name in violets.

To him no vain regrets belong
Whose soul, that finer instrument,
Gave to the world no poor lament,
But wood-notes ever sweet and strong.
Oh lonely friend, He still will be
A potent presence, though unseen,
Steadfast, sagacious and serene.
Seek not for him: he is with Thee.

35. A month after the death of his friend, Mr. Emerson wrote in his journal:—

"Henry Thoreau remains erect, calm, self-subsistent before me, and I read him, not only truly in his Journal, but he is not long out of mind when I walk, and, as to-day, row upon the Pond. He chose wisely, no doubt, for himself to be the bachelor of thought and nature that he was—how near to the old monks in their ascetic religion! He had no talent for wealth, and knew how to be poor without the least hint of squalor or inelegance. Perhaps he fell—all of us do—into his way of living without forecasting it much, but approved and confirmed it with later wisdom."

A little later Thoreau's family put his Journals into Mr. Emerson's hands for him to read. Their truth and beauty were a delight to him, and he felt that his friend had fully justified himself. He frequently came out of his study to read passages to the family. I find the following in his Journal for 1863:—

"In reading Henry Thoreau's journal, I am very sensible of the origin of his constitution. That oaken strength which I noted whenever he walked or worked or surveyed woodlots, the same unhesitating hand with which a field labourer accosts a piece of work, which I should shun as a waste of strength, Henry shows in his literary work. He has muscle and ventures on and performs feats which I am forced to decline. In reading him I find the same thoughts, the same spirit that is in me, but he takes a step beyond and illustrates by excellent images that which I should have conveyed in a sleepy generalization. 'T is as if I went into a gymnasium and saw youths leap, climb, and swing with a force unapproachable, though their feats are only continuations of my initial grapplings and jumps."

The friendship and honour one for the other ran true to the end, in spite of temperamental barriers in communication. Emerson spoke his feeling about his friend at the burial:—

"The Country knows not yet, or in the least part how great a son it has lost. It seems an injury that he should leave, in the midst, his broken task, which none can finish, a kind of indignity to so noble a soul that he should depart out of Nature before yet he has been really shown to his peers for what he is. But he, at least, is content. His soul was made for the noblest society; he had in a short life exhausted the capabilities of this world: wherever there is knowledge, wherever there is virtue, wherever there is beauty, he will find a home."